PRAYER
ANSWERS GUARANTEED!

FOREWORD BY BISHOP WALTER SCOTT THOMAS

Learn how to ask God...
and RECEIVE it!

PRAYER
ANSWERS GUARANTEED!
BISHOP GEOFFREY V. DUDLEY, SR., D.MIN.

Outskirts Press, Inc.
Denver, Colorado

Contents

WHAT PEOPLE ARE SAYING ABOUT PRAYER: ANSWERS GUARANTEED:

"Prayer is the channel to communicate with God in order to confess, make requests, get directions, gain strength, or to just be . . . Dr. G. Vincent Dudley provides a blueprint or road map to help the believer navigate through several of those areas of prayer. He also gives clear and helpful insights on how to engage in victorious warfare prayer.

If you want to grow in prayer, or get others you influence to develop a prayer life, this is a must read book. It is useful tool in a practical way. Literally, you are able to take the ideas and concepts, and in a practical way use them successfully throughout your Christian walk and journey.

Dudley simulates the desire to intimately want to be with a God who listens and wishes to answer prayers according to His will. This is a well written and conscious driven book that will continue to bless you as you glean its instructions. So, God's peace and good journey!"

Bishop T. Anthony Bronner
Senior Pastor
Elim Christian Fellowship
Founding Bishop
Turning the World Upside Down Covenant Fellowship
Buffalo and Rochester, New York

WHAT PEOPLE ARE SAYING ABOUT PRAYER: ANSWERS GUARANTEED:

"Prayer Answers Guaranteed speaks directly to the most overlooked element of prayer – Results! Too often Bible believing saints find themselves frustrated with God because their prayers are rarely answered. This work gives believers a biblical understanding to effectually fulfill the mandate God has given them. Bishop Dudley nails it! No more hoping and wishing – we must learn to both pray the Word and in the Spirit with full assurance of faith, knowing that God is a reward of them that diligently seek Him. A must-read for intercessors!"

+ J. Alan Neal
Ramstein-Miesenbach, Germany
European/Asian Regional Bishop
Full Gospel Baptist Church Fellowship, International

WHAT PEOPLE ARE SAYING ABOUT PRAYER: ANSWERS GUARANTEED:

"What a delight it was to read **Prayer Answers Guaranteed!** *As one who prays, I find this book to be an excellent tool, reminder and source of encouragement. I can see its use for new converts and believers, and as a new members' orientation, as a textbook, a "how to" book for instruction getting started in the spiritual discipline of prayer. I pray the body of Christ, the Church of Jesus Christ, embrace again prayer, communication (two-way) with the Almighty GOD!"*

Bishop Darryl D. Woodson
Adjutant-Bishop
Joint College of African-American Pentecostal Bishops
Pastor
El-Shaddai Pentecostal Church of Christ
Memphis, Tennessee

Foreword

Sometimes we forget that we are not in total control of all the things that happen in our lives. Our society teaches us to be *"captains of our own souls and master's of our own destiny."* Our educational system, our employment and career paths, have all been dedicated to one thing: mastery. It would be wonderful if we really could master everything that comes our way and handle each moment on the sole strength of our abilities and wisdom, but we can't. Life is bigger than the best of us. It is more powerful than we have ever expected, and it can devastate the strongest of individuals. Each day we see the parade of those who thought they could do it by themselves. Many are headed to jail, others to the graveyard, while others are still giving it one more shot at beating the system.

The truth is we need help. Bishop Geoffrey V. Dudley, Sr. understands this truth at a very deep, visceral, and personal level. He has seen the limitations that belong to us and he has seen the hand of God move to overcome them. For all we have going for ourselves, we are still *"our heavenly father's children,"* and there are times we do not possess the required abilities or wisdom to reach the God-appointed end. God has to step in, and God does.

PRAYER ANSWERS GUARANTEED!

In a season when so many are writing on how to build congregations, or how to develop youth ministries, Bishop Dudley has chosen to speak to the heart and soul of believers, and revive, reenergize, and reignite the real power of our faith and that is, our quality relationship with God. For Bishop Dudley, once we have consecrated that relationship, we see miracles start to happen all around us. The impossible is no longer impossible, because we are connected to the God who is Lord of all. His experiences have shared as the incubator for the ideas you will see presented here. He is no novice to this subject, nor is it academics without unction. This is his life, and he lays it open to us to glean from and to be blessed. Our prayer life is essential to this quality relationship. It is not a formulaic express that he is calling us into; rather, a personal, intimate communion with the one who is our best friend, our creator, and the lover of our soul.

If more believers understood the value and blessing of a quality prayer life, they would begin to know the joy the Lord promised. Prayer is communion communication. It is our phone call to the Eternal, our walk in the park with our God, and our stroll with the one who loves us more than anyone. Bishop Dudley is aware of this truth and lays it out in clear ways so every believer can become excited about time spent with God.

As you read this seminal work, be encouraged that your life is going to change and that a new wind is going to blow. It is the presence of the Holy Spirit and I promise you, you won't stop praying. Enjoy this work!

Bishop Walter Scott Thomas, Sr., D.Min.
Senior Pastor
New Psalmist Baptist Church
Baltimore, MD

Acknowledgments

I would like to acknowledge my administrator, Dagne, and her administrative team. Thank you for your tireless assistance in making this book a reality. Your tenacity and tremendous skills are priceless. I want to thank Deacon Pamela Dorsey, Chyriell Hill, and Nichole Islam for their meticulous editing. I want to thank my family: Glenda, the love of my life, Mahogany, and Geoffrey II. Your support and love makes me strong. I also want to acknowledge my parents. Had it not been for my father, Bishop Leamon Dudley, Sr.'s, stern and firm leadership, and my mother, the late Ida Dorothy Dudley's, powerful prayer life and encouragement, I would not be where I am today. Finally to my church, LifeChangers as we call ourselves, you are the greatest church a pastor could lead. I am honored and humbled by your followship.

Introduction

God is just a prayer away. All you need to do is call. He will hear your faintest cry. He's concerned about you, so while your tears are flowing through, your time of mourning. He is here to lift your heavy heart. Cause he is in love with you. He knows. He cares. He sees. He's there. And he'll carry you. He's concerned about you...
—CeCe Winans

We often overlook the privilege of prayer and forsake one of the most formidable weapons in the Christian's arsenal. Since we do not effectively, fervently, or consistently pray without ceasing, our lives are weaker and our victories over Satan are fewer. Many jettison prayer to the stockpile of, I tried it and it did not work, or it's too hard. We think a quick mutter to God will do it and we call it a day. Many may make the mistake of thinking – this book is going to be about the dull, difficult, dry subject of prayer. They fail to understand how prayer is often the missing link between being the Christian God wants them to be and the Christian they really are. Very simply, you will never fulfill your potential or plan God has for you without a powerful prayer life. Many people want to know how did we start a church with 28 and see it grow to over 2,300 in five years. Prayer was one of the main ingredients!

Prayer is so important. It is one of the seven principles of New Life in Christ Interdenominational Church (NLC). Progressive, proclamation, preparation, prayer, praise, perspective and prosperity are the principles on which the vision of NLC is built. They become the building blocks for the life-changing power within the believer. When you live by these principles, with the help of Christ, then you become a LifeChanger for life whether you are a member of NLC or not. When God gave me these seven principles for living, I believed they could change lives so much that I put them on the front of the church. Some have never paid the inscription any attention, just as they have never paid close attention to the power of prayer.

If you give this book your undivided attention, it will teach you how to pray to get answers – guaranteed. In particular, it will teach you the fundamentals of how to pray, hindrances to prayer, prayer that gets God's attention, the technique of praying the word, praying and fasting, praying in tongues, and defeating the enemy through prayer mapping.

Reading this book will change your prayer life forever. Reading this book will get you answers from God guaranteed! I know that is an audacious statement to make. I do not make it without a healthy dose of theological "fear and trembling". I am aware there is always the possibility of a book over-promising and under-delivering. To that end, I make the statement based on sound biblical study and theology. I do not make the statement based on a belief in a fancical "name it and claim it" theology, which is drawn from whimsical wishing. I also make the statement based on experiential data rooted in the day-to-day living of people like

INTRODUCTION

you and me. This book is drawn from a sermon series I preached that literally changed me and the church I pastor!

This book is written from the perspective that God desperately wants to communicate with humanity in general, and those who put their faith in him in particular. God desires to have a meaningful relationship with every believer, and relationships are built on continuous, effective, heartfelt communication. In other words, God is waiting to hear from you and anxious to answer you.

As you read this book and complete the study guide at the end of each chapter, you will be drawn into continuous effective, heartfelt communication with God. It will also have a true "prayermonial" from people who applied the prayer principle. These prayermonials will encourage you to apply the principles. When you do, I believe you will receive answers—guaranteed.

1

Fundamentals of Prayer

I'd rather be able to pray than be a great preacher; Jesus Christ never taught his disciples how to preach, but only how to pray.
—DL Moody

Every thought you think is a prayer. Every word you speak is a prayer. Every act in which you engage in is prayer because God's spirit lives in you.
—Author unknown

Are you ready for your life to explode? Did you know every explosion requires a fuse? Prayer is the fuse that lights the dynamite. However, prayer is not the first thing we think of when we think of explosions in our spiritual lives. And "pray tell" to coin a phrase, that is why many of our lives are lifeless and powerless. We do not pray. We are not unlike the disciples who asked Jesus to teach them how to pray. Someone said no great thing ever happened without it being preceded by prayer.

Prayer was the fuse that caused the church age to explode into existence. *Acts 1:14 says, [14]They all joined together constantly in prayer, along with the women and Mary, the mother of Jesus, and with his brothers.* Even though after Jesus' resurrection he repeatedly gave the disciples specific instruction to go to Galilee to receive power, that power was not released.

- *Mark 16:6-7: [6]"Don't be alarmed," he said. "You are looking for Jesus the Nazarene, who was crucified. He has risen! He is not here. See the place where they laid him. [7]But go, tell his disciples and Peter, 'He is going ahead of you into Galilee. There you will see him, just as he told you.'"*

It was not released and received until they prayed for ten days. Even though Jesus promised them the Holy Spirit would come, they still had to pray. After Jesus told them to pray, he ascended to heaven to receive their prayers for the first time as the resurrected Christ. The day the Holy Spirit came down from heaven is called Pentecost. Pentecost is a harvest festival. It was one of the five festivals set up by Moses under the law. It was the festival of God giving his word to Moses. Festival in Hebrew can be defined as a scheduled meeting or celebration. That means there was a scheduled time for the power of the Holy Spirit to abide with the disciples.

- *Acts 1: [8]But you will receive power when the Holy Spirit comes on you; and you will be my witnesses in Jerusalem, and in all Judea and Samaria, and to the ends of the earth."*
- *Acts 2:8-11: [8]Then how is it that each of us hears them in his own native language? [9]Parthians, Medes and Elamites; residents of Mesopotamia, Judea and Cappadocia, Pontus and Asia, [10]Phrygia and Pamphylia, Egypt and the parts of Libya near Cyrene; visitors from Rome [11](both Jews and converts to Judaism Cretans and Arabs—we hear them declaring the wonders of God in our own tongues!"*

FUNDAMENTALS OF PRAYER

The 120 still had to gather in the Upper Room and pray to ensure the preordained meeting and power would become reality. Notice how they were all in agreement with each other and the word of God. They also had been praying for a long time. This was also the first time we can infer their prayer was coed and not in the traditional Jewish way of separating the sexes in worship. They were physically in one place. When it finally happened, the Greek word for the explosion is *dumanous*. This is where we get the word dynamite!

- *Acts 2:²Suddenly a sound like the blowing of a violent wind came from heaven and filled the whole house where they were sitting.*

If they would not have prayed, there would not have been power to accomplish what Jesus commanded us to do. The gospel would have never have been launched to Judea, let alone into the uttermost parts. Given the fear of the disciples and their tendency to give into timidity when challenged with danger, they needed power to proclaim the gospel. Some say what gave the disciples boldness to die for Christ and proclaim he was Lord in the face of persecution was they had seen him after the resurrection. I want to add it was also because they had the power of the Holy Spirit. This was the preoccupation of Jesus' last conversation before he died and first conversation after his resurrection. The Holy Spirit would not have come with the requisite power for the apostles to plant churches all over the world and endure persecution unless there was first prayer.

We want the power. We want the explosive church growth and development of the early church. We want the miracles of the early church, but more often than not we do not dedicate our lives to the fundamental that make it all possible. Prayer. Prayer was the connection between promises made by God and promises kept by God.

It is time for you to find and use this weapon of mass destruction "WMD" – and blow Satan out of your lives. Satan is banking on you not reading this book. He is hoping you put this book beside the stack of books you plan to read. Then you will not learn what I am about to teach you. Satan wants to hold you captive to sadness, despair, defeat, poverty, powerlessness, sin, weakness, ignorance, and a life of mediocrity. Prove him wrong! Light the fuse and obliterate his power over your life.

As far back as I can remember prayer has been a part of my life. The youngest of 11, son of a preacher who pastored small rural churches early in his ministry, I remember hearing my parents' powerful prayers echoing through our house. That was commonplace. It seemed like trouble and struggle was always part of our lives and prayer was the anecdote. No matter what obstacles and problems the crucible of life created, I heard the constant refrain from my parents, "we need to pray", and "prayer can change things." Prayer became basic and fundamental to my being.

Every Sunday morning, with few exceptions, my family gathered around the table - with cold cereal waiting – to be led in prayer by my father. Before he started, my mother would mention several people who needed prayer. Without fail, we would say our Bible verses and my father would pray a prayer that warmed our souls, even though as a little boy, my concern was the cold cereal. Throughout the week, I remember people knocking on the screen door of our home in the projects. They would ask my mother, who would be standing at the stove cooking a big pot of pinto beans, to pray for them. At other times they would simply tell her "sister so and so or brother so and so" needs prayer. Whenever my parents had their friends over, and just before we would be told to leave the living room because "grown folk" were talking, as we left I would hear, "we need to pray for this or that." Little did I know I was learning the valuable lesson prayer is essential for living.

As that was my experience, I do not presume that everyone has been so fortunate or is so acquainted with prayer. To that end, please complete the following survey. This will help you assess your prayer life. It will also begin the process to give you some base knowledge you will need as you read the book. No matter your score, this survey will give you a sense of your knowledge of prayer and begin the process of how to pray to get answers guaranteed.

Pre-Test & Self Assessment

Before you can succeed in any worthwhile endeavor, you must master the fundamentals. In order to understand the fundamentals of prayer, <u>first you must determine what the fundamentals of your prayer life are?</u>

1. How long do you pray?
    a. 5 minutes a day
    b. 15 minutes a day
    c. 30 minutes a day
    d. an hour or more

PRAYER ANSWERS GUARANTEED!

2. How often do you pray?
   a. Daily
   b. Weekly
   c. Monthly
   d. Almost never

3. Write an answer you received to your prayers in the last year!

4. Do you pray in tongues/do you have a prayer language?
   a. If you do, write the scripture that authorizes you.

5. Name a prayer in the Bible other than the Lord's Prayer.

6. Who would you give the most credit for teaching you how to pray?
   a. mother
   b. father
   c. pastor
   d. Sunday school teacher

    e. sibling

    f. self taught

    g. other

7. List one scripture that mentions prayer other than the Lord 's Prayer.

8. What is Prayer?
    a. Prayer is communication with God
    b. a cry, a plea, a whimper, a praise, a wish
    c. Prayer is pillow talk, love chats, and an engagement with God
    d. Prayer is a desperate cry for help
    e. Prayer is a formal conversation with God
    f. All of the above

9. When does the Bible first mention prayer?

10. When should we pray?
    a. Morning
    b. Noon
    c. Night

    d. Before we eat

    e. All of the above

11. How should we pray?
    a. Standing
    b. Kneeling
    c. Walking
    d. Prostrate
    e. Eyes opened
    f. Eyes closed
    g. Does not matter

12. Is prayer still a requirement, since the Bible says God knows our needs before we ask?
    a. Yes
    b. No

13. The Lord's Prayer – fill in the blanks:

Our Father _____ _____ in heaven, _____ be thy name. Thy _____ come, Thy will _____ _____ on earth, as it is in _____. Give us this day our _____ _____. And forgive us _____ _____, as we _____ _____ debtors. And lead us _____ into _____, but deliver us from _____: For thine is the _____, and the _____, and the _____, forever. Amen.

14. Can prayer make God do something?
    a. Yes
    b. No

15. Is spiritual warfare still a reality today?
    a. Yes
    b. No

16. Do some prayers work better than others?
    a. Yes
    b. No

17. Is fasting and prayer still a viable option for believers?
    a. Yes
    b. No

18. Can you stop God from answering your prayers?
    a. Yes
    b. No

19. What is intercessory prayer?
    a. Prayer for healing
    b. Prayer for the nation
    c. Prayer for others
    d. Prayer for your specific need
    e. Prayer for your internal private needs

20. Do you have to be a believer to pray?
    a. Yes
    b. No

PRAYER ANSWERS GUARANTEED!

21. Match the six types of prayers with the scripture:

Prayer of Agreement (believers)	1. Phil. 1:3-4
Prayer of Faith (requesting, petition)	2. Luke 22:41-42
Prayer of Direction	3. Matt 18:19
i.　Two or more godly options	4. Luke 2:20-21
Prayer of Praise and Worship	5. Matt 18:18-19
i.　Thanks for what God has done	6. Mark 11:24
Prayer of Intercession (prayer for others)	
Prayer of Binding and Loosing (promises being released)	

Answers:

1) Unique to you	12) A
2) Unique to you	13) See Matthew 6
3) Unique to you	14) A
4) Romans 8	15) A
5) Jesus prayer in John	16) A
6) Unique to you	17) A
7) John	18) A
8) F	19) B, C
9) Genesis	20) A
10) E	21) A=3, B=6; C=2; D=4; E=1;
11) G	22) F=5

FUNDAMENTALS OF PRAYER

Study:

1. How do you feel about your answers?

2. Do you feel like you should have known more answers?

3. Which questions are you most bothered by not knowing?

4. What do you plan to do about the question(s) you don't know?

5. How would you rate your prayer life?
   a. Non-existent
   b. Poor
   c. Fair
   d. Good
   e. Excellent
   f. Outstanding

PRAYER ANSWERS GUARANTEED!

Prayermonial
(Testimony as a result of Prayer)

God's Word is true. God is good. God is master. In early February 2007, the doctor told me I had breast cancer. After about one minute of negative thoughts and an encroachment of fear and anxiety, I remembered who I am. I thought, "Wait a minute. You are a child of God. Jesus is my Rock. Jesus is my Lord, Savior, and friend. Helloooo. I laid a hand on myself and asked Jesus to help me and to heal me by His stripes. Before the diagnosis, I always knew that my God is awesome. I remained calm and assured that I would see total healing. I trusted Jesus. God caused me to open my mouth and tell certain people about the disease. I began to see them as God's helping hands. . . friends, ministry team members, and relatives, with all kinds of gifts, came to me right on time. While in the operating room before the anesthesia, I gathered the doctors, nurses, and technicians around me and prayed for a successful surgery and thanked the team for helping me. And I asked they let God lead them in their work on me. When the surgeon operated, he found that not only did the tumor shrink, but it was totally dead! Dead at the root! The doctor removed the small amount of shrunken dead tissue! Nothing is impossible for God! Nothing. Jesus healed me. He is so faithful and I am so grateful!

2

HINDRANCES TO ANSWERS TO PRAYER:
What's the Hold Up?

Satan rocks the cradle when we sleep off our devotions.
—James Hall
You can't use a prayer as a smokescreen to keep you from repentance.
—Adrian Rogers

Hindrances to prayer are probably the most overlooked area of prayer. More often than not, we look at God as the culprit behind our prayers not being answered. Rarely do we take an honest look at ourselves as a possible obstruction to stopping the answers to our prayer. I am reminded of a sermon a colleague of mine preached in which he told the true story of a couple who came to him for counseling. They were dumbfounded they were not receiving all the blessings he was preaching about and others were experiencing. They were beside themselves with frustration, and in disgust they exclaimed, "What could we possibly be doing wrong?" As he continued to ask them questions to get a better understanding of their lifestyle, they told him without hesitancy or a hint of repentance or shame, they were not married and were living together. It never crossed their minds their lifestyle was connected to their unanswered prayers. When confronted with the biblical truth about marriage, they had to choose between the lifestyle the culture has accepted as a new morality, or a biblical lifestyle that guaranteed answers to their prayers. They failed to understand the importance of *Proverbs 28:9*:

- *If anyone turns a deaf ear to the law, even his prayers are detestable.*

The Message Bible puts it even better:

- *God has no use for the prayers of the people who won't listen to him.*

God always wants to answer every plea for help from every believer, but the nature of God will not ignore certain things. God will not overlook disobedience, sin, unforgiveness, or a begging spirit just to answer your prayer, no matter how desperate your situation.

Needless to say, anything as needful and meaningful as prayer cannot exist without some opposition. In this chapter, I am going to address four hindrances to an effective prayer life. They are disobedience, secret sins, unforgiving spirit, and a begging spirit.

DISOBEDIENCE

Disobedience is a major hindrance to prayer. This is the main sin which broke up the fellowship between God and Adam. Someone said, "Sinning will stop us from praying, but more importantly, praying will stop us from sinning." Adam and Eve's communication with Satan was a form of prayer that corrupted their relationship with God. They stopped praying long enough to start sinning. Watchman Nee says, "Disobedience is not just another sin, it is the one sin that rebels against God."

We often view rebellion as a sin that is usually committed by unbelievers. Rebellion is one who refuses to act on the information which he/she received. However, if we dissect the word, we would discover that one would have to KNOW the law in order to rebel against it. Since it was the word preached to you that compelled you to believe in the salvation which saves you from your sins, when you disobey, you are rebelling against the word of God. God always acts against rebellion. Refusing to answer your prayers is just one way he shows his displeasure with rebellion.

When God speaks, he expects us to act on what he said. To do otherwise removes us from a state of dependence to a state of independence. When we are independent we tell ourselves we do not need God. Since by our actions we have told God we do not need him, God steps aside. God is not going to work against his own self-interests as detailed in his word. Therefore, rebellion becomes a defiant act of independence from needing God. If you do not need God, you do not need his answers to prayer. The children of Israel provide us with a very good example of rebellion.

- *Deuteronomy 1:42-45: And the Lord said unto me, Say unto them; Go not up, neither fight; for I am not among you; lest ye be smitten before your enemies. So I spake unto you; and ye would hear, but rebelled against the commandment of the Lord, and went presumptuously up into the hill. And the Amorites, which dwelt in that mountain, came out against you, and chased you, as bees do,* *and destroyed you in Seir, even unto Hormah. <u>And ye returned and wept before the Lord; but the Lord would not hearken to your voice, nor give ear unto you.</u>*

Because the children of Israel <u>didn't believe</u> what was said, this disbelief was treated as disobedience by God. God could not go with them to carry out his word. They didn't believe in God's word and they rebelled against it.

The children of Israel proved sin was not limited to smoking, drinking, adultery, lying, stealing, gambling, cursing, etc. Knowing what the Word of God says and refusing to act on it is also the sin of disobedience, which is rebellion.

- *James 4:17: Therefore to him that knoweth to do good, and doeth it not, to him it is sin.*
- *James 4:17: The Message - In fact, if you know the right thing to do and don't do it, that, for you, is evil.*

So when I refuse to do what I know is right I am sinning, and therefore God is not obliged to answer my prayer. Disobedience is one of the main causes for unanswered prayer.

Secret Sins

Nothing kills the joy of prayer like secret sin! When I speak of secret sins, I do not mean that God is unaware. God is aware of everything we do. Secret sins are the sinful habits believers practice while pretending, in words and deeds, to live a sinless life. Another way to describe secret sin is unconfessed sin. Secret sins originate in private; but, if allowed to go unchecked, it will be exposed in public.

Secret sin in our hearts is like the scum which clogs a pipe or gas line. It prevents the flow of the spirit. As believers, we must be quick to repent when we sin and not try to hide it. Don't be ashamed if you sin. Remember, no one is without sin. *1 John 1:8 says If we claim to be without sin, we deceive ourselves and the truth is not in us.* There are plenty, however, who are without repentance. In other words, when we know we are wrong, we should not seek to hide our wrong by making excuses! If you have hidden sin in your heart, your prayer life will be of no effect. That's why when we pray we need to submit our heart unto the Lord above all else. We cannot afford to allow secret sin to take residence in us. The Psalmist tells us what to do with our secret sin.

- *Psalms 19:12-14: Who can understand his errors? Cleanse thou me from my secret faults. Keep back thy servant also from presumptuous sins; let them not have dominion over me; then shall I be upright, and I shall be innocent from my transgression. Let the words of my mouth, and the meditation of my heart, be acceptable in thy sight, O Lord, my strength, and my redeemer.*

One of the most important elements of prayer is coming into the presence of God, bringing our sins with us, and then submitting them to him for cleansing.

Another result of secret sin is it severs relationships. Look at *Isaiah 59:22 But your iniquities have separated you from your God; your sins have hidden his face from you, so that he will not hear.* So many people think they are going to get God to do something when they have severed their relationship with him through their secret sin.

PRAYER ANSWERS GUARANTEED!

- *Ps. 66:18-18 If I had cherished sin in my heart, the Lord would not have listened;*
- *Prov. 1:28-30-28 "Then they will call to me but I will not answer; they will look for me, but will not find me. 29 Since they hated knowledge and did not choose to fear the LORD, 30 since they would not accept my advice and spurned my rebuke,*

Ask yourself this question: why would God answer your prayer for you to take his answer and continue living in sin. Our relationship with God is like the covenant marriage relationship between a man and a woman. Sin (an affair) breaks the relationship. What man would give a man money (answer to prayer) to sleep with his wife? You are in relationship with God, so why would God fund the demise of the relationship by answering your prayers. You only come home at night to eat, change clothes, and sleep (get your basic needs met), but you go out and enjoy life with your sinful lover. God is no fool.

A woman wrote the following letter to the editor of the *Miami Herald* after a hurricane passed through the area: "I never believed in God or prayer. I thought it was superstition, but the storm was coming and I thought I'd see if it really works. I asked God to protect my house and my house got damaged. All these people say they believe in God and believe in prayer. What do you say about that?"

The editor's answer was great: "Madam, I don't know much about prayer either, but it must be that God was busy taking care of his regular customers."

HINDRANCES TO ANSWERS TO PRAYER

An Unforgiving Spirit

Any time we allow unforgiveness, ill feelings, resentment, bitterness and grudges to enter our heart, we are warned by the word of God that our prayers will not be heard.

- *Matthew 5: 23-24: "Therefore, if you are offering your gift at the altar and there remember that your brother has something against you, 24 leave your gift there in front of the altar. First go and be reconciled to your brother; then come and offer your gift. NIV*

The offering is to the priest so he can intercede for you. Sin stops the offering and therefore the intercession. Final result: no prayer…no answer, due to sin. Unforgiveness will constipate a child of God so that nothing spiritual will flow through him/her. Jesus declares that if we do not forgive from the heart, we will be dealt with severely by our Heavenly Father.

- *Mark 11:25-26: And when you stand praying, forgive, if ye have ought against any; that your Father also which is in heaven may forgive you your trespasses. But if ye do not forgive, <u>neither will your Father, which is in heaven, forgive your trespasses.</u>* (emphasis mine)
- *Luke 11:4: And forgive us our sins; for we also forgive every one that is indebted to us.*

Begging Spirit

Begging will not produce answers to prayer! Let's hear what Dr. Luke has to say.

- *Luke 11:8; 18:5: ⁸I say unto you, Though he will not rise and give him, because he is his friend, yet because of his importunity he will rise and give him as many as he needeth. ⁵Yet because this widow troubleth me, I will avenge her, lest by her continual coming she weary me. KJV*

We commonly think this story's central theme is to nag the person long enough and you will get results. In fact, the text seems to say as much...because this widow troubled me or because of the importunity of the person wanting bread...The text also says:

- *Luke 11:9,10 : ⁹And I say unto you, Ask, and it shall be given you; seek, and ye shall find; knock, and it shall be opened unto you. ¹⁰For every one that asketh receiveth; and he that seeketh findeth; and to him that knocketh it shall be opened. KJV*

Notice how the first letters of the three verbs actually spell ask (ask, seek, knock). The three verbs are even in the aorist tense, which means to continue to do until there is a response. However, begging will not produce an answer. The key word importunity does not mean to beg. Begging God will not make God do something just as a child begging a parent for something will not make the parent give in. More often than not, crying spells and temper tantrums result in certain disciplinary measures otherwise known as a good ole-fashion spanking. In this case, begging only produces more crying and praying the spanking will stop.

Emotions alone do not move God. God cares. God is aware of our tears. The Psalmist says in Psalms 56:8 - *Record my lament; list my tears on your scroll — are they not in your record?* But God does not answer because God sees tears. Did Abraham begging God to stop destroying Sodom and Gomorrah stop him? Abraham asked God at least six times to spare Sodom. Begging will not produce a breakthrough.

More often than not, begging comes from someone who may be attempting a shortcut – a child will beg for something even though the parents have said you won't get it unless... Begging also comes from people who do not know their rights. Begging generally comes from someone with a poverty spirit. I am not just talking about financial poverty, but spiritual poverty. Begging is the by-product of an individual who does not fully understanding how to ask God for something God really wants to do. A begging spirit unwittingly tells God you don't trust him. It creates doubt. Begging comes from an inner belief that the person has what you are asking for, but does not want you to have it. God wants to answer you so your persistence in prayer (importunity) should be:

a) Reminding God of his word
b) Thanking God for the answer
c) Agreeing with God the answer is coming
d) Asking God for his joy and strength until the answer comes
e) Looking for additional scripture to go to God in prayer.

Never beg. When I was a child, my parents used to tell me – don't beg, you are a Dudley. We are children of the King – King's kids don't beg.

Once in church I walked up to a person while I was teaching Bible study on prayer and demanded they give me $100. The church was aghast. The atmosphere became tense. The person gave me the $100. What everyone didn't know is that I had given the person the $100 before church began to make the point. The money was mine, so I had the right to demand it. You don't have to beg when you know the answer belongs to you!

I will discuss more about begging God in the next chapter. The bottom line is, God is not going to be used by anyone. God does not answer prayers to further your flesh or ignorance in how to pray. You must be bound to him as a bondservant. Unforgiveness, unconfessed sin, and living in disobedience and disconnected to God will <u>not</u> produce answers from God.

- *Prov. 6:16-19: There are six things the LORD hates, seven that are detestable to him: 17 haughty eyes, a lying tongue, hands that shed innocent blood, 18 a heart that devises wicked schemes, feet that are quick to rush into evil, 19 a false witness who pours out lies and a man who stirs up dissension among brothers.*
- *Prov. 6:16-19: THE MESSAGE - Here are six things God hates, and one more that he loathes with a passion: eyes that are arrogant, a tongue that lies, hands that murder the innocent, a heart that hatches evil plots, feet that race down a wicked track, a mouth that lies under oath, a troublemaker in the family.*

God will not hate something and then turn around and bless it. You may ask what about all the people you see sinning and seemingly getting answers to prayer? When those who practice sin seemingly get their prayers answered, it is because someone else who could get a prayer answered was interceding for them in prayer. It was not because God ignored sin.

HINDRANCES TO ANSWERS TO PRAYER

Prayermonial

One day as I was leaving the casino, as I just finish paying more rent so the boat could float, there laid on the floor a one hundred dollar bill. Crazy, I'm thinking this was a blessing! So little-o-happy me went back to the casino some days later and security saw me on camera, came over to introduce themselves, asked me to watch their video of me removing paper from their floor, and asked if I'd reported it (no). Long story short, I received a letter in the mail from the court system which stated that since I did not report finding money, that they would be charging me with stealing. I retained an attorney for three times as much as I had found that day and was ordered to pay two times as much on top of that as a court fine for not reporting found money on their property. (KJV) The Word-Ecclesiastes 7:5. It is better to hear the rebuke of the wise (Pastor/First Lady/Husband), than for a man/woman to hear the song of fools. James 1:13-14. Let no one say when he is tempted, "I am tempted by God"; for God cannot be tempted by evil, nor does he himself tempt anyone. But each one is tempted when he is drawn away by his/her own desires and enticed. When this all started, my husband and I begin to sing this song of praise and pray. When all of this was over, I continued to thank the Lord and never went back on my word to stay clear of that evil place. The Lord then showed me a real blessing by blessing me with a job promotion from supervisor to general manager, which I did not even ask for, and I was also called with the increase of my work in the church to include hospitality and greeting services. Now I will continue to only serve one master. I thank God for all his love and kindness of mercy towards my judgment on desire which led me astray. When there was sin in my life, he heard my prayer, but did not answer. Once I let go of the sin, he blessed me.

PRAYER ANSWERS GUARANTEED!

Chapter Study Guide:

1. Are you willfully practicing sin?
    a. Yes
    b. No

2. Are you disobeying God's word?
    a. Yes
    b. No

3. Do you have unforgiveness, bitterness, or anger in your heart for someone?
    a. Yes
    b. No

4. Do you have unconfessed, secret sin in your life?
    a. Yes
    b. No

If you answered yes to any of the previous questions, you are stopping your guaranteed answers to prayer. Confess your faults according to John 1:9 by listing them. Ask God to forgive you. If possible, go to anyone who has offended you, or whom you have offended, and ask for forgiveness.

3

Prayer that Gets God's Attention

Heaven is full of answers to prayers for which no one ever bothered to ask.
—Billy Graham
Prayer doesn't need proof, it needs practice.
—Author Unknown

There is a story that is told about the prayer of Bill Moyer who was on President Lyndon Johnson's cabinet. President Johnson asked him to lead the Cabinet in prayer before they began their meeting. As Bill Moyer, at that time a Baptist minister, prayed, President Johnson said, "Speak up; we can't hear you." Moyer reportedly said, "Excuse me, Mr. President, but I wasn't talking to you." Bill Moyer only needed the attention of God. His audience was an audience of one.

When you pray, remember you only need the attention of one. In order to get God's attention keep in mind a couple of things and apply some basic principles. Remember, God wants to be in a relationship with you. Remember, relationships require communication. Prayer in its simplest form is communication. God is waiting to hear from you. Finally, since God knows relationships flourish when there is two-way communication,

PRAYER ANSWERS GUARANTEED!

God must answer to keep the lines of communication open. Knowing what gets God's attention can be seen in four basic principles: 1) God listens to his word, 2) God pays attention to your posture, 3) Faith is fundamental to prayer and, 4) God is just. These principles are illustrated in the life of several biblical characters that I will use as examples of how they prayed and got God's attention.

Remind God of What He Said

The first basic principle to getting God's attention is to say what God has said. God pays attention to what he said. In other words, pray prayers from the Bible that God has answered before. Find prayers in the Bible that biblical characters prayed and whose situation and request is similar to yours. Pray those prayers for your situation. Prayer is your privilege, so take advantage of it, especially since God expects to hear from you. The characters in the Bible were not different from you. With all their faults, hardships and trials, they prayed. They prayed and got tremendous results. Why? How? James puts it this way:

- *James 5:13-18: ¹³Is any one of you in trouble? He should pray. Is anyone happy? Let him sing songs of praise. ¹⁴Is any one of you sick? He should call the elders of the church to pray over him and anoint him with oil in the name of the Lord. ¹⁵And the prayer offered in faith will make the sick person well; the Lord will raise him up. If he has sinned, he will be forgiven. ¹⁶Therefore confess your sins to each other and pray for each other so that you may be healed. The prayer of a righteous man is powerful and effective. ¹⁷Elijah was a man just like us. He prayed earnestly that it would not rain, and it did not rain on the land for three and a half years.* ^{18}*Again he prayed, and the heavens gave rain, and the earth produced its crops.*

The most encouraging part of that verse is Elijah was a man just like us. One of the most inspiring elements of prayer is God's promise to hear and answer the call of his children. There is no question about him hearing. The Psalmist makes it even clearer:

- *Psalms 4:3: But know that the Lord hath set apart him that is godly for himself; the Lord will hear when I call him.*

It is important that we know, when one of God's children cries, he or she immediately gets God's attention. Getting God's attention – his immediate attention – doesn't mean you will get an instant answer. This is where our faith takes over and whether we are living a godly life. We must know he hears and will answer.

It is to our advantage to impregnate our hearts with the promises of God so that when we pray, we use his words with confidence. Then we will know that he will hear and answer. Praying and receiving answers will stimulate our praying more than anything else. It is to our advantage to seek God's face for answers on a regular basis, because each answer we receive will prepare us for the next level.

- *Psalms 18: In my distress I called upon the Lord, and cried unto my God; He heard my voice out of his temple, and my cry came before him, even into his ears*
- *Proverbs 15:29: The Lord is far from the wicked; but he heareth the prayer of the righteous*

- *Micah 7: Therefore I will look unto the Lord; I will wait for the God of my salvation; my God will hear me*

Moses Reminds God of What He Said

At the apex of God's anger at the quarrelsome unbelief of the children of Israel, Moses refreshed God's memory about his promise to the forefathers of the Israelites.

- *Numbers 14:10-16, 20: ¹⁰ But the whole assembly talked about stoning them. Then the glory of the LORD appeared at the Tent of Meeting to all the Israelites. ¹¹ The LORD said to Moses, "How long will these people treat me with contempt? How long will they refuse to believe in me, in spite of all the miraculous signs I have performed among them? ¹² I will strike them down with a plague and destroy them, but I will make you into a nation greater and stronger than they." ¹³ <u>Moses said to the LORD</u>, "Then the Egyptians will hear about it! By your power you brought these people up from among them. ¹⁴ And they will tell the inhabitants of this land about it. <u>They have already heard that you</u>, O LORD, are with these people and that you, O LORD, have been seen face to face, that your cloud stays over them, and that you go before them in a pillar of cloud by day and a pillar of fire by night. ¹⁵ <u>If you put these people to death all at one time,</u> the nations who have heard this report about you will say, ¹⁶ '<u>The LORD was not able to bring these people into the land he promised them on oath</u>; so he slaughtered them in the desert.'" ²⁰ The LORD replied, <u>"I have forgiven them</u>, as you asked."*

Moses simply reminded God of what God's plans were for the future of his newly-chosen people. God could not go back

PRAYER THAT GETS GOD'S ATTENTION

PRAYER THAT GETS GOD'S ATTENTION

on his stated position. According to Jeremiah 29:11, God has plans for you. God has no intentions of ignoring his plans for your life. Remember:

1. He will never leave you.

   - …Joshua 1:9: *Have I not commanded you? Be strong and courageous. Do not be terrified; do not be discouraged, for the LORD your God will be with you wherever you go.*

2. He will not put more on you than you can bear.

   - …1 Cor. 10:13: *[13]No temptation has seized you except what is common to man. And God is faithful; he will not let you be tempted beyond what you can bear. But when you are tempted, he will also provide a way out so that you can stand up under it.*

3. He will provide for you.

   - …Ps. 37:25 :*[25] I was young and now I am old, yet I have never seen the righteous forsaken nor their children begging bread.*

Remind God of His Justice

Let's look at Luke 18:1-8 so you can see more clearly how you get God's attention - *[1]Then Jesus told his disciples a parable to show them that they should always pray and not give up. [2]He said: "In a certain town there was a judge who neither feared God nor cared about men. [3]And there was a widow in that town who kept coming to him with the plea, 'Grant me justice against my adversary.' [4]"For some time he refused. But finally he said to himself, 'Even though I don't fear God or care about men, [5]yet because this widow keeps bothering me, I will see that she gets justice, so that she won't eventually wear me out with her coming!' "[6]And the Lord said, "Listen to what the unjust judge says. [7]And will not God bring about justice for his chosen ones, who cry out to him day and night? Will he keep putting them off? ⁸I tell you, he will see that they get justice, and quickly. However, when the Son of Man comes, will he find faith on the earth?"*

Importunity is persistence. Persistence is not begging; persistence is insisting you get what belongs to you. God is always on the side of the oppressed. God is a God of justice. The widow was oppressed by an unfair justice system. She demanded her rights and got them. The fallen state of the world has created an unjust system against marginalized people and believers. When they cry out, God will respond.

Remind God of Your Humility

You should watch your posture, and ensure pride and pretension do not enter the room. For example:

- Luke 18:10-14: *¹⁰"Two men went up to the temple to pray, one a Pharisee and the other a tax collector. ¹¹The Pharisee stood up and prayed about himself: 'God, I thank you that I am not like other men--robbers, evildoers, adulterers--or even like this tax collector. ¹²I fast twice a week and give a tenth of all I get.' ¹³But the tax collector stood at a distance. He would not even look up to heaven, but beat his breast and said, 'God, have mercy on me, a sinner.' ¹⁴I tell you that this man, rather than the other, went home justified before God. For everyone who exalts himself will be humbled, and he who humbles himself will be exalted."*

God does not want you to come to him prideful and pretentious. God is turned off by someone who projects themselves as someone important by comparing themselves to others.

I remember when I was in the Air Force stationed at Hancock

Field in Syracuse, NY. Since I was from North Carolina, we drove I-95 South through Richmond, Virginia to go home for the holidays. Every year I would see the Virginia Union University Seminary exit sign. Since I could remember, I always wanted to attend seminary. I prayed with persistence that God would orchestrate my life so I could go to that seminary. In nine years of praying persistently to go to Virginia Union, God miraculously used a base closure, me failing to get promoted, and an assignment away from my family for one year to get me to that seminary.

Hancock Field closed by order of Congress. I was reassigned to Griffiss AFB, Rome, New York, a few miles north. The supervisors were extremely racist and made sure I would not get promoted to the easiest rank in the AF: captain. This caused a delay in a new assignment to Germany. I was miraculously promoted six months later and reassigned to Osan AB, Korea, for one year. That assignment made it possible for me to be assigned to Hampton, Virginia, where I was able to commute to VA Union Seminary for its non-traditional hour weekend program.

No other sequence of events could have gotten me to Virginia. Had I gone to Germany, it would have been for three years. Prayer ordered each step. I was persistent, because I knew the call on my life needed seminary to fulfill God's plan for me. I could demand it, because I knew I would be used to minister to marginalized people. I was humbled through the entire process, because the failure to get promoted humiliated me.

Request the Spirit to Pray

- Romans 8:26 & 27: *[26]In the same way, the Spirit helps us in our weakness. We do not know what we ought to pray for, but the Spirit*

himself intercedes for us with groans that words cannot express.
[27]And he who searches our hearts knows the mind of the Spirit,
because the Spirit intercedes for the saints in accordance with God's
will.

It is important your prayers be consistent with what the Holy
Spirit would pray for you. In other words, due to our human
frailties and weaknesses, we are unable to clearly articulate our
precise needs all the time. When that happens, the Spirit of God,
which resides in every believer, prays on our behalf. This prayer
is exactly what one needs, but is unable to say. When the spirit
prays for you, through you, then the will of God for your life is
requested by the Spirit and answered by God. God does not turn
down his Spirit. I will talk more about prayer language in chapter
six.

Prayer that Glorifies God and Furthers God's Agenda

- 1 Kings 18:41-46: *[41] And Elijah said to Ahab, "Go, eat and
  drink, for there is the sound of a heavy rain." [42] So Ahab went
  off to eat and drink, but Elijah climbed to the top of Carmel,
  bent down to the ground and put his face between his knees. [43] "Go
  and look toward the sea," he told his servant. And he went up and
  looked. "There is nothing there," he said. Seven times Elijah said,
  "Go back." [44] The seventh time the servant reported, "A cloud as
  small as a man's hand is rising from the sea." So Elijah said, "Go
  and tell Ahab, 'Hitch up your chariot and go down before the rain
  stops you.'" [45] Meanwhile, the sky grew black with clouds, the wind
  rose, a heavy rain came on and Ahab rode off to Jezreel. [46] The
  power of the LORD came upon Elijah and, tucking his cloak into*

PRAYER THAT GETS GOD'S ATTENTION

his belt, he ran ahead of Ahab all the way to Jezreel.

Elijah's prayer was answered because his prayer glorified God. Glorifying God simply means making God look good. Remember, James said Elijah was a man just like you and I. When our prayers are in line with God's agenda, our prayers will get God's attention. When our prayers are to make God look good, it is just a matter of time before God answers them.

Hezekiah is another example of prayer that glorifies God and advances God's agenda. *Isaiah 38:1-8: 1 In those days Hezekiah became ill and was at the point of death. The prophet Isaiah son of Amoz went to him and said, "This is what the LORD says: 'Put your house in order, because you are going to die; you will not recover.'" 2 Hezekiah turned his face to the wall and prayed to the LORD, 3 "Remember, O LORD, how I have walked before you faithfully and with wholehearted devotion and have done what is good in your eyes." And Hezekiah wept bitterly. 4 Then the word of the LORD came to Isaiah: 5 "Go and tell Hezekiah, 'This is what the LORD, the God of your father David, says: I have heard your prayer and seen your tears; I will add fifteen years to your life. 6 And I will deliver you and this city from the hand of the king of Assyria. I will defend this city. 7 This is the LORD's sign to you that the LORD will do what he has promised: 8 I will make the shadow cast by the sun go back the ten steps it has gone down on the stairway of Ahaz.' " So the sunlight went back the ten steps it had gone down.*

Hezekiah, whose name means God is my strength, was approximately 39 years old when we come to chapter 38. He has been the king of the southern kingdom (Judah) for about 14 years. His total reign is 29 years, so he is about half way through his kingship. Jerusalem was under siege. Syria attacked Jerusalem and put a blockade around it because Israel owed the

Syrian king back taxes. This same king has already taken control of the northern kingdom of the 10 tribes of Israel. Not only are the Israelites in trouble over back taxes, the root problem was the condition of their spiritual relationship with God. Hezekiah's sickness (he had boils all over his body) was the manifestation of Jerusalem's sickness. Jerusalem was spiritually sick from head to toe with sin. Jerusalem will be devastated and likewise Hezekiah is going to die, but something happens. He prayed – he prayed a prayer that got God's attention. James 5:17 states when you are in trouble you should pray. In this text Hezekiah is in trouble. The prophet Isaiah showed up to pronounce that he should make funeral arrangements, because Hezekiah was going to die. When the text says he should get his house in order, the Hebrew phrase means for him to find a man to carry out the King's destiny. It means he should put Israel's governmental affairs in order. Instead of giving up and accepting death, the text says he rolled over and prayed.

I'd say Hezekiah was in trouble and it was time to pray. After all not only did his pastor tell him he was going to die, he told him you will not recover. How would you feel if your pastor came to your house and told you what Isaiah told Hezekiah? Maybe you have not been told that, but you have received devastating news or been confronted with difficult times and want to know what kind of prayer can get God's attention. You may not have had to hear what Hezekiah heard, but you have heard something that broke your heart: I don't love you any more…I hate you, Mommy…we have to let you go…etc. There will be times in our lives when the news we receive or the situation we experience may leave us feeling as though there is no hope – like Hezekiah. But hope is not lost. God gave us a precious gift in the story of

Hezekiah. Like peering through a department store window and looking at something you always wanted, but didn't know if you could afford it, God lets us know answers to prayer is attainable by leaving us the example in Hezekiah's prayer. His prayer gives us insight as to how prayer works. So what is it about his prayer that got God's attention?

His Prayer Heartfelt & Sincere

The text states God saw Hezekiah's tears as well as listened to his prayer. That says a lot. It tells me God was looking and listening to Hezekiah's heart. The Hebrew for the word tears in this context means to embrace and weep. There are times when your prayers must embrace God through a heart that is turned inside out. Tears are messages from the heart. Your tears do not go unnoticed by God Remember *Psalms 56:8: Record my lament; list my tears on your scroll - are they not in your record?*

God is not moved by your tears, but follows your tears to see inside your heart.

His Prayer Had Feet on It

vs. 21 - *Isaiah had said, "Prepare a poultice of figs and apply it to the boil, and he will recover."* Hezekiah actually had to do something to receive his complete healing. By applying feet to his prayer, he applied a home remedy on his boils. Prayer without feet cannot deliver an answer from God. You can pray for a job, but until you get up and look for one, you probably will not get one. You can pray that your children do better in school, but until you spend time with them helping them with homework, your prayer probably won't get answered.

His Prayer was Backed up with a Life of Faithfulness

vs. 3 *"Remember, O LORD, how I have walked before you faithfully and with wholehearted devotion and have done what is good in your eyes."* Hezekiah was a faithful man and was noted by scholars as one of Israel's best kings. His prayer came from a lifetime of living for God. History tells us Hezekiah had taken Israel through spiritual reforms. He had torn down the high places and cleansed the Temple so they could worship there again. He even tore down the serpent that Moses had used in the wilderness, because they had become fixated on the symbol and not the God behind the symbol. All of these acts demonstrated his faithfulness to living a life pleasing to God.

Hezekiah's Prayer had Purpose

Hezekiah's prayer got God's attention because he had the powerful purpose of defeating the Syrians who had put a blockade around the city.

- Your prayer must have a purpose that furthers the kingdom agenda of God. In other words, it must be in the will of God. It was the will of God to save Jerusalem, but God was willing to let Jerusalem be defeated, just like he was going to allow Hezekiah to die if he had not prayed a prayer that had purpose. That tells me some things will happen that are not the will of the God unless someone prays with purpose.
  » Your prayer cannot be selfish.
  » Your prayer life cannot be all about you.

We often overlook that God told Hezekiah "to put his house

PRAYER THAT GETS GOD'S ATTENTION

in order". The Hebrew for that phrase means God did not have a son to carry out the Davidic kingdom. Until Hezekiah could get a son to ensure the Davidic Kingdom would continue, he could not die. So Hezekiah reminded God about that in his prayer. The government affairs could not be put in order without a son to carry on his legacy. His healing furthered God's agenda, because God promised the kingdom of David would never end. Hezekiah's prayer had purpose.

God Answered Hezekiah with:

- **A Word**
  - » vs. 4, 5, 6: *Then the word of the LORD came to Isaiah:* [5] *"Go and tell Hezekiah, 'This is what the LORD, the God of your father David, says: I have heard your prayer and seen your tears; I will add fifteen years to your life.* [6] *And I will deliver you and this city from the hand of the king of Assyria. I will defend this city.'"*

Answered prayer more often than not will come in the form of a word. You must be attentive and alert to hear, because many times God speaks in a still quiet voice. He will use his word to tell you what to do. Remember, God doesn't have idle conversations, so your undivided attention is important.

- **A Sign:**
  - » Vs. 7, 8: [7] *"'This is the LORD's sign to you that the LORD will do what he has promised:* [8] *I will make the shadow cast by the sun go back the ten steps it has gone down on the stairway of Ahaz.' "So the sunlight went back the ten steps it had gone down.*

Other times God speaks with a sign. For Hezekiah, God moved the sundial back 10 hours. In other words, the day went in reverse by 10 hours so Hezekiah would know God was going to do what he said. Your sign that your prayer got God's attention may not be that dramatic so again, be alert and pay attention. Your sign will be a sense in your spirit.

- **A Response:**
  - » vs. 5: *"Go and tell Hezekiah, 'This is what the LORD, the God of your father David, says: I have heard your prayer and seen your tears; I will add fifteen years to your life.'"*

God finally gave him more than what Hezekiah asked for. Not only did he save his life, he extended it. What manner of man is this that can receive devastating news like that and instead of falling apart, he prays? I believe he was a man of like passions just like James said of Elijah. He was a man of like passion like you and I. James 5:17 in the Message bible: *The prayer of a person living right with God is something powerful to be reckoned with. Elijah, for instance, human just like us, prayed hard that it wouldn't rain, and it didn't—not a drop for three and a half years. Then he prayed that it would rain, and it did. The showers came and everything started growing again.*

It isn't the man; it is the prayer in the man or woman that gets God's attention. What kind of prayers are you praying?

Prayermonial

On Monday, my daughter was rushed to the hospital because she had a severe headache and could not speak. The MRI revealed that she had a lesion on her brain and the blood cells surrounding the lesion had burst, causing blood on her brain. We had faith and knew she had great purpose, and her destiny had not been fulfilled. We contacted others to agree in prayer. We prayed and we reminded God of these things. The head neurosurgeon there performed another MRI and an angiogram to see how much damage had been done to her brain. Her father anointed the left side of her brain with oil and we continued to pray for her. By the miraculous power of Jesus and the grace of God, she is speaking and was released from the hospital. SHE IS A LIVING TESTIMONY!!! She is now at home and regaining more strength day by day. She should have been dead, paralyzed, or had a stroke based on the diagnosis. Prayers of the righteous got God's attention.

Chapter Study Guide:

1. Do you pray to get God's attention?
   a. Yes
   b. No

2. Do you pray to get man's accolades or material gain?
   a. Yes
   b. No

3. Do you know God's agenda for the issue you are praying about?
   a. Yes
   b. No

4. Do you know the plan God has for your life?
   a. Yes
   b. No

5. What is God's agenda for your life? Hint: It should glorify God (make God look good, not you).

6. Find scriptures and promises from God to match God's agenda for your life and begin asking God to fulfill his agenda by positioning you, prospering you, and preparing you.

Write your prayer here:

4

Praying the Word

The Word of God represents all the possibilities of
God are at the disposal of true prayer.
—AT Pierson
Prayer that gets to heaven is prayer that starts in heaven.
—Adrian Rogers

By now you may have noticed something while reading this book. When it comes to getting answers from God, knowing God's word is paramount. Each chapter up to this point has used God's words to guarantee answers from God. Using God's words in your prayer life is one of the most powerful tools in your arsenal of prayer. Using God's words enables you to stay focused. It keeps you from praying from your emotions. It prevents you from trying to pray like the old deacon in a traditional Baptist church or other "influential people" in your life. You may remember, Sunday morning the chairman of the deacon board would say wonderful melodious words and phrases in his prayer that ended pretty much the same way: "when we get to the Jordan River…" Those prayers had their place, even though they were prayers meant more for man's ears than God answering them.

PRAYER ANSWERS GUARANTEED!

This chapter will cover extensively the principle of praying God's word. Failure to pray God's word will greatly reduce your chances of getting your guaranteed answers from God.

Prayers that guarantee answers require an above-average knowledge of the word. You may say that you don't possess that kind of knowledge. This is a good place to start. The way to start is simply to look in the concordance of your Bible for the word that matches your prayer request. This will lead you to several verses that may correspond with the issues you are praying about. You can also buy books on the promises of God. Use those promises to begin to formulate your prayer request. Be as specific as possible when using the word or God's promises. The more precise you are, the more you give God to work with and it will be easier to recognize the answer when it comes. When you pray you must be precise. Most of our prayers are bland and vanilla. Bless them. Bless me. Help them. Help me. Heal them. Heal me. It is in your best interest to be specific. When you shop for clothes, groceries, etc., you don't waste time looking for things not on your list. When children ask parents for something, they are exact. I want a cookie, a car, money, or whatever they desire. To do otherwise would not get them what they wanted. You also must follow the rules. When you play a sport, you use the rules for that sport not the rules of another sport. E.g. football has it rules – you don't use basketball rules to play football.

- *James 4:2-3: ²You want something but don't get it. You kill and covet, but you cannot have what you want. You quarrel and fight. You do not have, because you do not ask God. ³When you ask, you do not receive, <u>because you ask with wrong motives</u>, that you may spend what you get on your pleasures.*

PRAYING THE WORD

In other words, James is saying there are rules when you pray; your motives must be clear, pure and consistent with God's will. If not, you do not receive what you ask. When you pray God's word, you need to know the following:

Understand the Power of God's Word

- *Psalm 119:89: Forever, O LORD, thy word is settled in heaven.*

The Hebrew for settled in this context, means established deputy or appoint. When we take God at his word, God deputize and appoints us to carry out his word as an agent of Heaven. Now we have the powerful word of God to use in prayer.

- *Isaiah 40:8, KJV: The grass withereth, the flower fadeth, but the word of our God shall stand forever.*
- *Isaiah 40:8, THE MESSAGE: These people are nothing but grass, their love fragile as wildflowers. The grass withers, the wildflowers fade, if God so much as puffs on them. Aren't these people just so much grass? True, the grass withers and the wildflowers fade, but our God's Word stands firm and forever.*
- *Matthew 24:35: Heaven and earth shall pass away, but my words shall not pass away.*

The Power of the word penetrates areas that emotional prayers fall short.

- *Hebrews 4:12-13: God means what he says. What he says goes. His powerful Word is sharp as a surgeon's scalpel, <u>cutting through everything, whether doubt or defense</u>, laying us open to listen and* *obey. Nothing and no one is impervious to God's Word. We can't get away from it—no matter what. MSG*

Words are so powerful in a court of law they carry the penalty of perjury when they are untrue. Swearing is an assurance. When you are unable to guarantee, you solicit someone who can insure you carry out your promise e.g., "Do you swear to tell the whole truth and nothing but the truth." You don't swear because you cannot guarantee your word. God's word is so powerful he can only use himself to verify it's truthfulness.

- *Hebrews 6:13,14: When God made his promise to Abraham, since there was no one greater for him to swear by, he swore by himself, saying, "I will surely bless you and give you many descendants."*

You have to be able to take God at his word or everything about God crumbles. When you cannot take a person's word the relationship is immeasurably affected. Remember, God's word is at stake; it isn't about you it is about God's word, his glory, and his reputation.

Prayermonial

There is power in agreement and spiritual authority. Greetings! I just wanted to let you all know how very thankful I am for you all being such a big part of my life. If you all remember, when Bishop began to teach us about the power of agreement, I asked you all to stand in agreement with me that I would one day meet the father I have never met. You all prayed with me and for me that I would one day meet my father. There is power in agreement. After 35 years of going through many, many things drawing closer to God and my purpose in him and much prayer, his word was made manifest in and thru me. I departed on Monday the 27th of October to Accra, Ghana, West Africa, to honor the grandfather I never knew and to meet the father I've never known. BUT GOD! Only God knows how much this means to me and I thank you all so much for your prayers and support. Look what God will do when we all get on one accord! We serve a BIG God everyone. Nothing is impossible for him, nothing! [When you stand on his word.]

Answers: Prayer Bound by the Word

Once you pray God's word, the power of his word is activated to be carried out. One of the major failures in prayer is when we do not pray the word. We pray for things that are not in the Bible and not the will of God for our lives. We pray for financial blessings when we don't tithe. We pray for healing while we still eat an unhealthy diet. Our prayer should be Lord give me the discipline to tithe, exercise and eat right, and use your free will to do so. We pray for Johnny to obey, quit selling drugs, come home, and do better in school. We should be praying a word of salvation over Johnny's life. Find the scripture you need by going to your concordance and matching your situation with the word.

- *Exodus 33:12,13,17: Moses said to the LORD, "You have been telling me, 'Lead these people,' but you have not let me know whom you will send with me. You have said, 'I know you by name and you have found favor with me.'…Remember that this nation is your people." And the LORD said to Moses, "I will do the very thing you have asked, because I am pleased with you and I know you by name."*

PRAYER ANSWERS GUARANTEED!

Moses prayed for The Children of Israel. Moses needed to remind God of God's word concerning the children of Israel. Moses found the word God promised to bless Abraham to be a great nation. God had to carry out his word.

God's word must abide in you.

- *John 15:7: If ye abide in me, and my words abide in you, ye shall ask what ye will, and it shall be done unto you.*

Abide means to dwell, to be attached to; when you are attached, you repeat the sap of the word that flows through the vine. You must have faith in God's word.

- *Hebrews 11:1: Now faith is the substance of things hoped for, the evidence of things not seen.*

The Hebrew word for substance is setting, the same as the word being established or set in heaven in Ps. 119:89. Faith then is the establishment or setting of the word in you. Faith is anchored in the substance of God's word. When you have little knowledge of the word, the result is thereby having very little substance for faith to anchor itself in. Additionally, you will have little faith to pray the word and believe. If you violate the word by living a sinful lifestyle, you deteriorate the confidence you have in the word by your behavior, because if you had confidence in the word, you would obey it and not sin. If you had confidence in the word, you would live it. Your behavior would reflect it. Your refusal to live the word corrupts your confidence; in turn your faith fails, because your confidence collapses under the weight of sin. So when John says, "This is the confidence we have that when we pray…" you don't have any confidence, so you are without faith to get an answer.

- *Romans 10:17, KJV: So then faith cometh by hearing, and hearing by the word of God.*
- *Romans 10:17: THE MESSAGE: Isaiah asked what we all ask at one time or another: "Does anyone care, God? Is anyone listening and believing a word of it?" The point is: Before you trust, you have to listen. But unless Christ's word is preached, there's nothing to listen to.*

The word is established in you by hearing the word. When it is set in you or established in you, then your faith grows. Faith grows by the amount of word you hear and obey, so when you pray his word it has been established in you and established in heaven. Therefore, you just repeat what is established in you and heaven.

- *Matthew 18:18,19,20: 18 Verily I say unto you, Whatsoever ye shall bind on earth shall be bound in heaven, and whatsoever ye shall loose on earth shall be loosed in heaven. 19 Again I say unto you, that if two of you shall agree on earth as touching anything that they shall ask, it shall be done for them of my Father which is in heaven. 20 For where two or three are gathered together in my name, there am I in the midst of them.*

This is a scripture affirming the legality and lethality of God's word. Jewish law required two or three witnesses to establish truth/word of truth. When you agree with God's word, and ask others to agree with you about a prayer request, you are not only receiving more faith to bring about an answer, you are legally binding God to carrying it out. You and others become a force multiplier to the legality, lethality and truth of God's word. Faith is increased similar to if everyone in the church gave one dollar of faith to add to my dollar of faith. The strength of my dollar is the same, because it is still worth a dollar. But the <u>ability</u> of my dollar to do more has increased because other dollars were added to it. So it is with adding my faith to the word and agreeing with others. Here is a real life story that gives an even clearer picture of what it means when you are connected to others in prayer and agreement.

Prayermonial

I arrived in August of 06 and went to the Men of Valor retreat. At that time, I was looking for jobs and took a night maintenance job that did not pay much. In January when Pastor taught about first fruits, I knew I didn't have the money for giving first fruits and keeping up with my bills, etc., but I just began to save up a dollar here and a dollar there for it. I gave my first fruits. I had prayed that I would get a job that would help me keep up with my bills and pay my tithes, so I was putting in for this job and that job. On April 17th I received a call to talk to a gentleman about a job where I did not even apply! When I arrived, there were two people waiting – and he told me up front they had already substituted for the exact job that I was about to interview for. After the interview, he asked me was I connected to New Life, and I said yes. On the way out, he walked past the two others that were waiting and told his asst principal (also a LifeChanger) to tell them there was no need to wait, he found the man for the job, and hired me on the spot! When I went to try to give the other job notice, the general manager asked if I would stay and they would work around my new job, because they didn't want to lose a good worker — so that would be the answer to another prayer! A couple of months into the new job, the assistant superintendent called me and said that I was being paid the wrong thing. I thought they meant they had been paying me too much, but in fact, they were paying me at a step 1 and they said, "We want to pay you for step 3," which was for people with three years experience that I did not have! On top of that, he said that in 2008 I would move to the step 4 — even more blessings. Since I joined this church and began to live the word as I am being taught by Pastor Dudley, my blessings have overtaken me! I will look any man in the face with pride and tell them — I love my Pastor. I absolutely thank God for you and First Lady!

Big Things...Big Answers

- *Eph 3:20: Now to him who is able to do immeasurably more than all we ask or imagine, according to his power that is at work within us.*

There are times we could get more from God, but we are limited by the word we know, so we refuse to ask for big things. Our prayers are rarely for big things. We don't think big. We limit God because of a lack of faith. We assume God will not change things for us. Listen to Moses' prayer to God not to destroy the Israelites. This was a BIG request to say the least:

- *Deut. 9:25-29: 25 I lay prostrate before the LORD those forty days and forty nights because the LORD had said he would destroy you. 26 I prayed to the LORD and said, "O Sovereign LORD, do not destroy your people, your own inheritance that you redeemed by your great power and brought out of Egypt with a mighty hand. 27 Remember your servants Abraham, Isaac and Jacob. Overlook the stubbornness of this people, their wickedness and their sin. 28 Otherwise, the country from which you brought us will say, 'Because the LORD was not able to take them into the land he had promised them, and because he hated them, he brought them out to put them to death in the desert.' 29 But they are your people, your inheritance that you brought out by your great power and your outstretched arm."*

Moses believed God for big things. Moses believed his prayers could change things. They did. Look at what God did when members at my church needed big things from God.

Prayermonial

I am an anesthesiologist and was involved in a case in the operating room in July 2001. It was a case involving a young lady for a routine procedure that should have lasted 20 minutes. However, during the procedure there were problems with the patient's heart rate and blood pressure. At the point when the patient was most critical, the surgeon called me to the room where I gave two drugs that increased her heart rate and blood pressure. I was called too late to correct the problem, so the patient remained in a coma due to a lack of oxygen to the brain. The hospital and nurse anesthetist settled the case by paying a very large sum of money; however this settlement could not be disclosed at the trial. During the course of their settlement, my family and I were fasting and praying that I would be removed from the case and God answered our prayers. God has a way of changing the atmosphere even in the courtroom. In the lawyer's efforts to make me look bad, God had a way of letting the jurors see the truth of the situation. The jurors found us not guilty of all the charges. They even said that I was a hero in the case and had saved the patient's life. Even during the reading of the verdict there was a spiritual atmosphere in the courtroom as we were praising and thanking God for the victory. Again, God showed Himself to be true to His word. I came into agreement with my pastor and my church family on my victory, and God came through with his promises!

You cannot go wrong praying the word. As a starter guide, here are some scripture prayer starters. **(found on www. praythescriptures.com)**

Prayer Promises

- *Jer 1:12...I am ready to perform My Word.*
- *Jn 16:24...Ask, and you will receive, that your joy may be full.*
- *Mt 21:22...whatever things you ask in prayer, believing, you will receive.*
- *Jer 33:3...Call to Me, and I will answer you, and show you great and mighty things...*
- *Jn 14:14...If you ask anything in my name, I will do it.*

Praying for Relationships

- *Mt 21:21...Father, I come before You in prayer and in faith.*
- *Rom 13:11...Your Word says that now is the time for all to awaken from sleep,*
- *Rom 13:11...For our salvation is nearer now than we first believed.*
- *Col 1:13...Lord, deliver my loved ones from the power of darkness,*
- *Rom 13:12...and cause them to put on the armor of light.*
- *Rom 13:14...Help them in their daily walk to put on the Lord Jesus Christ*
- *Rom 13:13...and to avoid the lusts and idolatry of life.*

PRAYER ANSWERS GUARANTEED!

- *Ps 119:37...Cause them to turn their eyes away from worthless things,*
- *2Tim 2:26...to come to their senses, and escape the snare of the devil.*

Scriptures for Healing

- *Hos 4:6...My people are destroyed for lack of knowledge.*
- *Gal 3:13...Christ has redeemed us from the curse of the law, having become a curse for us...*
- *1Pet 2:24...Jesus bore our sins in His own body on the tree, that we, having died to sins, might live for righteousness -- by whose stripes you were healed.*
- *Isa 53:5...He was wounded for our transgressions, He was bruised for our iniquities; the chastisement for our peace was upon Him, and by His stripes we are healed.*
- *Mt 8:17...He Himself took our infirmities and bore our sicknesses.*
- *Ps 107:20...He sent His word and healed them, and delivered them from their destructions.*

Praying for the Children

- *Acts 19:20...I thank you, Father, that Your Word prevails over our children.*
- *Isa 54:13...That they are taught of the Lord and continue to be*
- *Prov 13:1... the fruit of godly instruction and correction.*
- *2Tim 1:9...Father, You have saved them and called them with a holy calling,*
- *2Tim 1:9 ...not according to works, but according to Your own purpose.*

PRAYING THE WORD

- *2Tim 4:18...Deliver them from every evil work and preserve them.*
- *John 10:5 ...They will by no means follow strangers, not knowing their voices.*
- *Prov 2:6... Father, give us counsel and wisdom in bringing up our children.*
- *1Pet 2:2... desiring the pure milk of the Word that they may grow thereby.*
- *Jas 1:19...That they are swift to hear, slow to speak, and slow to wrath.*
- *Heb 13:5... and they are content with what they have.*
- *2Pet 3:18... I pray that they grow in the grace and knowledge of our Lord,*

Scriptures for Encouragement

- *1Sam 12:16...stand and see this great thing which the Lord will do before your eyes...*
- *Luke 18:27...The things which are impossible with men are possible with God.*
- *Num 23:19...God is not a man, that He should lie. Has He said, and will He not do it?*
- *Jas 1:4...But let patience have its perfect work, that you may be perfect and complete, lacking nothing.*
- *Rom 8:31...If God be for us, who can be against us?*
- *2Tim 2:1...be strong in the grace that is in Christ Jesus.*

Praying for the Church

- *Matthew 16:18...That thou art Peter, and upon this rock I will build my church; and the gates of hell shall not prevail against it.*
- *Heb 10:22...Let us draw near to You with a true heart in full*

assurance of faith,
- *Col 3:16...Let Your Word dwell in us richly.*
- *Col 1:10...that we may live and conduct ourselves in a manner worthy of You,*
- *Col 1:10...fully pleasing You.*

Chapter Study Guide:

1. How often do you study/read the Bible?
   a. Daily
   b. When I am in church
   c. Weekly other than church attendance
   d. Monthly
   e. Almost never

2. How often do I commit scripture to memory?
   a. Never
   b. Rarely
   c. Seldom
   d. Often
   e. Daily

3. Write your most important prayer request using God's words. Pray this prayer until God answers. Remember, written prayers list your request by needs that are associated with the word. Written prayers are precise, focused and are not emotionally dependent.

5

Fasting and Prayer:
2 Weary 2 Pray...2 Desperate 2 Stop

Prayer is reaching out and after the unseen; fasting, letting go of all that is seen and temporal. Fasting helps express, deepens, confirms the resolution that we are ready to sacrifice anything, even ourselves to obtain what we see for the Kingdom of God.
—Andrew Murray

If you want to hear from God, turn your plate down.
My mother—Ida Dorothy Dudley

When I was a teenager, I was often asked to preach in the local churches in my community. I was too young to drive, but old enough to realize the importance of preaching powerful messages from God. So, I believed I needed to fast and pray before each sermon. Somehow, I knew if I was going to be effective, I had to fast and pray. In fact, I'd fast all day Saturday and Sunday until after I finished preaching. I would not eat or drink. I did that because I remember my mother saying if you want something from God you had to fast and pray. She would say, "You need to turn your plate down and pray." I desperately wanted to preach well, so the key to success for me was a lifestyle of fasting and prayer. Even as a teenager, it became second nature. In this chapter you will learn how to fast and pray mainly through looking at the life of several biblical characters.

Today, fasting and praying is a lost spiritual discipline in the church. In the onslaught of "name it and claim it" theology, fasting and praying seems like it is too much trouble and sacrifice. Even though the Bible is full of instances when individuals and the nation of Israel were called to fast and pray, food has always been used to increase the faith of God's people. God told Israel they were not supposed to live by bread alone, but by every word that preceded out of his mouth. Then God gave them manna.

- *Exodus 16:32: Moses said, "This is what the LORD has commanded: 'Take an omer of manna and keep it for the generations to come, so they can see the bread I gave you to eat in the desert when I brought you out of Egypt.'"*

Why did God do that? He did it to show them he would always provide, but bread was not their sustenance for living – he was. So whenever they would fast it would be an act of trusting God not an attempt to manipulate God. We see that in the following biblical examples.

Daniel

First there is Daniel, who went on what is commonly called a "Daniel Fast". It was not an absolute fast. He refrained from eating specific foods so as to remain pure for godly service. He fasted and prayed for the trials he would have to endure in the Lion's Den.

- *Daniel 6:10: 16 [10] Now when Daniel learned that the decree had been published, he went home to his upstairs room where the windows opened toward Jerusalem. Three times a day he got down on his knees and prayed, giving thanks to his God, just as he had done before. [16] So the king gave the order, and they brought Daniel and threw him into the lions' den. The king said to Daniel, "May your God, whom you serve continually, rescue you!"*

Then he fasted and received revelation to lead his people.

- *Dan. 1:8; 9:3; 10:3: [8] But Daniel resolved not to defile himself with the royal food and wine, and he asked the chief official for permission not to defile himself this way. [3] So I turned to the Lord God and pleaded with him in prayer and petition, in fasting, and in sackcloth and ashes. [3] I ate no choice food; no meat or wine touched my lips; and I used no lotions at all until the three weeks were over.*

The first thing you see with Daniel is fasting was a way of life for him. He did not only fast and pray when times were desperate; he fasted and prayed as a routine. Fasting is going without some or all food or drink, or without some or all activity in your life. Fasting doesn't convince God you are serious about your prayer life, it convinces you. It is not starving yourself. Isaiah reminded the Israelites that fasting meant prayer-changed behavior. Isaiah wanted to remind them fasting and prayer was not a dietary issue, but an issue of personal deliverance from a lifestyle not pleasing to God. He wanted them to know when done correctly, fasting will have results in the way you live.

- *Isaiah 58:3-7: ³ 'Why have we fasted,' they say, 'and you have not seen it? Why have we humbled ourselves, and you have not noticed?' "Yet on the day of your fasting, you do as you please and exploit all your workers. ⁴ Your fasting ends in quarreling and strife, and in striking each other with wicked fists. You cannot fast as you do today and expect your voice to be heard on high. Is this the kind of fast I have chosen, only a day for a man to humble himself? Is it only for bowing one's head like a reed and for lying on sackcloth and ashes? Is that what you call a fast, a day acceptable to the LORD? ⁶ "Is not this the kind of fasting I have chosen: to loose the chains of injustice and untie the cords of the yoke, to set the oppressed free and break every yoke? ⁷ Is it not to share your food with the hungry and to provide the poor wanderer with shelter— when you see the naked, to clothe him, and not to turn away from your own flesh and blood?*

Fasting is a form of denial. It is a spiritual discipline practiced to raise your spiritual antennae to better hear from God. Spiritually there are times when you are in a dead zone. You can't get any reception – your calls keep dropping. The only way you can establish and maintain communication is fast and pray. Daniel fasted regularly and God always responded. Once he responded immediately:

- *Daniel 9:20-23: 20 <u>While I was speaking and praying</u>, confessing my sin and the sin of my people Israel and making my request to the LORD my God for his holy hill. <u>21 while I was still in prayer, Gabriel, the man I had seen in the earlier vision, came to me in swift flight</u> about the time of the evening sacrifice. 22 He instructed me and said to me, "Daniel, I have now come to give you insight and understanding. 23 As soon as you began to pray, an answer was* *given, which I have come to tell you, for you are highly esteemed. Therefore, consider the message and understand the vision."*

Another time it took him some time:

- *Daniel 10:12-13: 12 Then he continued, "Do not be afraid, Daniel. <u>Since the first day</u> that you set your mind to gain understanding and to humble yourself before your God, your words were heard, and I have come in response to them. <u>13 But the prince of the Persian kingdom resisted me twenty-one days.</u> Then Michael, one of the chief princes, came to help me, because I was detained there with the king of Persia.*

Esther

Esther called the whole nation of Israel to fast and pray.

- *Esther 4:16: "Go, gather together all the Jews who are in Susa, and fast for me. Do not eat or drink for three days, night or day. I and my maids will fast as you do. When this is done, I will go to the king, even though it is against the law. And if I perish, I perish."*

The very survival of the Israelites was on the line. After they fasted and prayed, God gave Esther the nerve and the favor to go before the king. Prayer and fasting saved the day. It could save your day!

Jehoshaphat

Jehoshaphat fasted and prayed to win the battle.

- *2 Chronicles 20:3: Alarmed, Jehoshaphat resolved to inquire of the LORD, and he proclaimed a fast for all Judah.*

After the people fasted and prayed ,they received revelation as to how to fight the battle. The way to win the batter was to put Judah first! That answer did not come until they fasted and prayed.

Ezra

- *Ezra 8:23: So we fasted and petitioned our God about this, and he answered our prayer.*

Ezra called a fast because he realized it would take more than ingenuity to reconstruct the wall and Temple.

Nehemiah

- *Nehemiah 1:4: When I heard these things, I sat down and wept. For some days I mourned and fasted and prayed before the God of heaven.*

Fasting and prayer was a part of extraordinary task of reconstructing the Temple and walls of Jerusalem. It took more than brick and mortar to rebuild; it took fasting and prayer.

Jesus

Jesus fasted and even said some things would not happen, except one fasted and prayed for them to happen.

- *Matthew 4: After fasting forty days and forty nights, he was hungry. NIV*
- *Mark 9:29: And he said unto them, This kind can come forth by nothing, but by prayer and fasting. KJV*

He even gave instruction to those doing it for the wrong reasons and the wrong way:

- *Matthew 6:16: "When you fast, do not look somber as the hypocrites do, for they disfigure their faces to show men they are fasting. I tell you the truth, they have received their reward in full. NIV*

When you fast and pray, you need to have a plan. It is not to be done haphazardly. The following are some guidelines.

Preparation for Fasting

1. Begin drinking plenty of water; squeeze fresh lemon juice in your water.
2. Begin cutting back the caffeine and sugars; drinking plenty of water will help you get over the cravings for caffeine, sugar and carbonated drinks.
3. Slowly reduce your solid food intake over several days.
4. Increase your liquid intake.
5. Determine whether you will do an absolute fast or Daniel fast.

Types of Fasting

There are at least two known fasts in the Bible.
1. The Absolute Fast (Matthew 4:2)

PRAYER ANSWERS GUARANTEED!

This is a total fast, which includes complete refraining from food or drink for the duration of the fast. (Best done after following preparation steps 1-5 above)

2. The Partial Fast (Daniel 10:3)
   This fast is from particular food or things that hinder our spiritual growth.

Breaking Your Absolute or Partial Fast

1. Please do not eagerly seek to eat everything you want at one minute past midnight on the final day of the fast. Slowly break the body in.
2. Begin with soft foods that are not heavy, such as Jell-O, applesauce, etc. Do this for a day or two.
3. Continue drinking plenty of liquids; water is recommended.
4. Once you feel your body has adjusted, begin eating small quantities of a healthy diet.

NOTE: Fasting is not a diet or weight reduction plan. Consult your physician before you fast if you are on any medications or required to eat for other health reasons (diabetics, etc.).

When life gets desperate and your emotions get the best of you, it is probably time to fast and pray. Jesus said there are times when this combination is the only thing that can arrest answers from heaven and give you strength to overcome. Often it is when you are too tired to pray and too desperate to stop. One real life example took place at New Life.

FASTING AND PRAYER

Prayermonial

Have you ever wondered why God does the things he does and it makes us hurt, or so we think it hurts. God does things to bring us closer to him so that He may receive the Praise, Glory, and the Honor for ALL to see. If God never made us uncomfortable, why would we draw closer to him when everything is going good? Well, God surely drew me closer to him during my divorce. I could not understand why God permitted so much hurt in my life. In the Fall of 2006, after a tumultuous marriage and later divorce, I was thrown out of my house by my ex-husband and my kids were taken from me. I was homeless and awarded weekends with my own children! Then God whispered to me, "Don't worry about those three children; I got them. You go about my work and give your time, talent and treasures." There is no need to guess how high my faith meter was registering by Jan '07. My faith in God was pretty high. I gave my 1st Fruits. I wasn't sure how I would do it, but God said, "Just do it. I will give it back." And I have not wanted for anything. When I was put out, I carried only what I could get in a Black Hefty Trash Bag and moved into an apartment. The apartment stay was supposed to be temporary. The stay turned out to be a year plus, but God was faithful and restored what was lost. The custody part of the divorce was resolved to joint custody in Sep '07. On Dec 28, I closed escrow on the purchase of my own condo! I give God All the Praise, Glory and Honor. Remaining faithful to God, prayer and fasting works! I am thankful for family, dear friends, pastor and 1st Lady & LifeChangers for all their fasting, prayers and encouragement who prayed, cried, talked, listened, laughed and hugged me and the children throughout.

PRAYER ANSWERS GUARANTEED!

Chapter Study Guide:

1. How often do you fast and pray?
2. Have you ever fasted and prayed?
3. If you answered yes to question 2, how long and what was the <u>result?</u>

4. What is the difference between an absolute fast and a "Daniel" fast?

5. Pick a period of time when you will fast and pray.
6. Pick a particular prayer petition you wish to pray.
7. Journal when you start, when you finish, and when your prayer is answered.

8. Be sensitive to the Holy Spirit. If you sense God telling you to fast and pray, know Satan would not suggest that. If you pray and fast remember to be precise with your prayer, the time, the cause and journal.

6

Prayer Language:
Praying and Speaking in Tongues

Groaning which cannot be uttered are often prayers which cannot be refused.
—CH Spurgeon
Prayer obtains and contains fresh well outpourings of the Spirit.
—JC Ryle
Where there is much prayer, there will be much of the Spirit; where there
is much of the Spirit, there will be ever-increasing prayer.
—Andrew Murray

One cold December night my mother called me into her room and told me we had to pray for one of my brothers. I was no more than thirteen at the time. I had given my life to Christ at age 12 and started preaching the next year. My brother was in his early twenties. My immediate thought was how could I pray for my brother. I remember thinking I was too young and why was my mother including me in this prayer? She had never done that before. When she told me what we were going to pray about, I became even more afraid and began to feel completely powerless. My brother had a heroin habit that was fast becoming an addiction. He worked in Washington, DC, and was late returning to work from the holidays. He told my mother he needed bus money. At that time, the Greyhound was the main mode of travel between Goldsboro, NC and Washington, DC. He also told my mother he feared when he got back, he would lose his job. He was desperate. My mother, as usual, seemed to think prayer could solve everything. I wasn't so sure, since I had seen my brother, through the crack in the bathroom door, shoot heroin into his veins a few months earlier and there was no sign he had stopped. My mother was not discouraged. She said, "Son, lay your hands on your brother. We are going to pray." She got some consecrated olive oil and anointed my brother's forehead. She began to pray. I tried to pray. My mother prayed like I'd never heard her pray before. My brother began to jump and shout in my parents' small bedroom. My mother began to speak in tongues and so did my brother. I was quiet and frightened. I had never heard my mother speak in tongues (pray in her prayer language). I had never seen my brother act like that before. Growing up in a holiness church I'd heard about people speaking in tongues and praying in a prayer language, but I had never witnessed it. We went to church on Sundays from sun up to well into the night. We <u>had</u> to go to revivals. But in all my church going, I had never heard anyone speaking in tongues. Now I was hearing it for the very first time. My brother eventually stopped and so did my mother. He left. He caught the bus. He kept his job. Today, after a lot of ups and downs in life, Larry is a powerful preacher.

That experience convinced me of the authenticity of praying in the spirit or what is commonly called praying in a prayer language. It is important for you to know there is a difference in speaking in tongues and praying in tongues, or what is also called praying in your prayer language. Praying in tongues is direct communication to God. It is communication encrypted and deciphered by the

Holy Spirit for the express purpose of sharing your innermost desires that cannot break through the interference your flesh sometimes presents. This especially happens during stressful, hopeless, and desperate times in your life. During these times if you start praying and do not edit your words, more often than not your words, tears, and expressions will turn into prayer language. Paul says it this way in *Romans 8: 26,27: In the same way, the Spirit helps us in our weakness. We do not know what we ought to pray for, but the Spirit himself intercedes for us with groans that words cannot express. [27] And he who searches our hearts knows the mind of the Spirit, because the Spirit intercedes for the saints in accordance with God's will. The Message Bible makes it even clearer. [26] Meanwhile, the moment we get tired in the waiting, God's Spirit is right alongside helping us along. If we don't know how or what to pray, it doesn't matter. He does our praying in and for us, making prayer out of our wordless sighs, our aching groans. [27] He knows us far better than we know ourselves, knows our pregnant condition, and keeps us present before God.*

In order to understand praying in tongues, one must understand some basic facts.

a. Praying and speaking in tongues by any other name is still communication.

b. It is communication that cannot find voice any other way, like laughter and crying. Both are ways to communicate a reality that cannot be communicated clearly other than the utterance of laughing or crying.

c. There are two schools of thought on tongues. One is it ended in the church age when it served its purpose, and the other is it is a gift, like other gifts, still in operation today. It is just like the gift of helps, hospitality and other gifts found in Romans and Corinthians, which believers possess and use today, so is tongues.

Paul refers to tongues in 1 Co. 12:28-30 and lists it as a gift. It is impossible to single out one gift as fulfilling its requirements in the body of Christ while others have not. Those who believe that do so out of blindly holding onto their dogma and ignoring the phenomenon of individuals experiencing supernatural communication with God. They also often, and I believe wrongly, quote 1 Cor. 13:8, which says *(KJV) ⁸Charity never faileth, but whether there be prophecies, they shall fail; whether there be tongues, they shall cease; whether there be knowledge, it shall vanish away.* They fail to read verse 10: *But when that which is perfect is come, then that which is in part shall be done away. KJV*

They fail to see when the text refers to tongues ceasing in the context of referring to when Jesus returns and we are in heaven. At that point, there will not be a need to communicate with God in that manner, because we will be with him.

   d. The express purpose of tongues is for communication to God problems that naturally, due to emotions or other limitations, would not be communicated by the person praying.

Remember the premise of prayer is to communicate to God, who wants to be in relationship with you, and realizes answering you opens up the lines of communication. For that reason, when you cannot pray as you should, God intervenes spiritually to keep the lines of communication open. When that happens, we speak in tongues. Paul even said he wished everyone would speak in tongues.

PRAYER LANGUAGE

- *1 Corinthians 14:5: I would like every one of you to speak in tongues, but I would rather have you prophesy. He who prophesies is greater than one who speaks in tongues, unless he interprets, so that the church may be edified.*

If you do not speak in tongues or have a prayer language, remember it is like any language. It is developed over time and practice. A baby starts communicating with one-syllable words and increases with maturity. So it is in your Christian walk. If you desire to speak in tongues and have a prayer language, ask God for the gift. When you sense an unintelligible word coming out of your mouth during a heart-wrenching prayer or praise, do not edit it or stop it. It is natural to want to understand what you are about to say. That is why it is supernatural when you speak in tongues, because it is inarticulate at the moment you speak. The more you speak each word; your speech will lead to another one. Sometimes God will tell you what you said. Other times someone else may interpret your words. If there is no interpretation, then you should pray in tongues at home, as it is for your own edification. This is according to *1 Cor 14:27-28. If any man speak in an unknown tongue, let it be by two, or at the most by three, and that by course; and let one interpret. 28 But if there be no interpreter, let him keep silence in the church; and let him speak to himself, and to God.*

Prayer language is a precursor to spiritual warfare, which is what you will learn in the next chapter.

Prayermonial

I am thankful for another year with Jehovah Shalom. HIS Faithfulness keeps me PRAISING HIM! I PRAISE GOD that our son accepted

Christ this year…what a witness of the power of the WORD! Our oneness has elevated our marriage to a place where GOD truly rests and our home is blessed. The women's ministry challenged me to reach out to my sisters this year and I did! I adopted the theme…I will NOT grow without my sister and I didn't. During the weekend of the 24-hour prayer in preparation for the Deliverance service on Sunday, I thought it would be short and sweet. NOT!!! At midnight, my body began to show the effects of fatigue. I remember grabbing the pole on the lower level and clinging to it, and crying out to GOD not for me, but for the body of Christ. At this point, I don't remember feeling fatigue or much of anything else after that. Next thing I knew it was 2:00 a.m.! GOD moved mightily in me because I prayed for the entire four hours! After this I had a greater desire for my prayer language and I asked GOD for it. It was birthed on August 23rd around 2:00 a.m. after the WoV Prayer Vigil! I am finally walking in my calling and my gifts at NLC, and now I truly am PRAISING HIM!

Chapter Study Guide

1. Have you ever spoken in tongues?
   a. Yes
   b. No

2. Have you ever felt or sensed the urge to speak in tongues while praying or praising God?
   a. Yes
   b. No

3. Do you have a desire to speak or pray in tongues?
   a. Yes
   b. No

4. Have you ever uttered words while praying or praising that seemed unintelligible to you?
   a. Yes
   b. No

Self Help Hints:

The Bible says in Acts 2:4, *⁴All of them were filled with the Holy Spirit and began to speak in other tongues as the Spirit enabled them.*

The Bible also says in *1 Corinthians 14:32, The spirits of prophets are subject to the control of prophets.*

To that end, speaking in tongues and praying in tongues is prompted by the Holy Spirit and released or stopped by the individual. So when you sense unintelligible words about to come out of your mouth, or sense them within yourself, open your mouth. One-syllable words may be all you speak at first. If you continue to open your mouth at those precise moments, then your words will lengthen. Remember, you are communicating with God now. Ask for the interpretation or wait for someone else to interpret. It is supernatural, so don't be afraid. Trust the supernatural God you love.

7

Prayer as a Weapon for Spiritual Warfare: Prayer Mapping

Is your prayer your steering wheel or your spare tire?
—*Corrie ten Boom*

A church without an intelligent, well organized and systematic prayer program is simply operating a religious treadmill.
—*Paul E. Billheimer*

When I was 18 years old, I remember that I accidentally went into my parents' room without knocking. It was early in the morning and my parents were preparing to take me to college. When I opened the door I saw something I had not seen before. My mother was on her knees on the side of her bed praying. I knew my mother prayed, so seeing her pray was not a surprise. Seeing her prostrate, vulnerable and so dependent on God completely humbled me. I grew up in a time when children were not allowed to see crying or weakness in their parents. My eyes watered and I quietly stepped back, and have never forgotten that morning. I had seen the prayer warrior at war and the battle was too much to comprehend. Somehow I knew she was battling for me, because I was the youngest of 11 and the last to leave home. I was on my way to college, never to return as her baby boy. I didn't know the battles that lay ahead of me, but she did, so she started claiming spiritual territory on my behalf. She was a modern day Daniel. She was conducting spiritual mapping. Let me explain. A deeper look into the life of Daniel and Balaam will reveal the biblical principle of spiritual mapping, also known as prayer mapping. Prayer mapping is strategically using prayer as a weapon in spiritual warfare.

Daniel, Satan and Michael in Spiritual Mapping

- *Daniel 10:12-14: Then he continued, "Do not be afraid, Daniel. Since the first day that you set your mind to gain understanding and to humble yourself before your God, your words were heard, and I have come in response to them.* [13] <u>*But the prince of the Persian kingdom resisted me twenty-one days.*</u> *Then Michael, one of the chief princes, came to help me, because I was detained there with the king of Persia.* [14] *Now I have come to explain to you what will happen to your people in the future, for the vision concerns a time yet to come." NIV* emphasis mine

In this famous text, we see the spiritual principle of prayer mapping being practiced by Satan who had assigned one of his strongest demons over the geographical locale of Persia. This location was where God's chosen people were held in bondage. Satan was not about to permit their physical or spiritual freedom without a fight. Prayer mapping is based on the premise that we wrestle not against flesh and blood, but against a distinguishable chain of command of evil demonic spirits led by Satan.

PRAYER AS A WEAPON FOR SPIRITUAL WARFARE

- *Ephesians 6:12: For we wrestle not against flesh and blood, but against <u>principalities</u>, against <u>powers</u>, against the <u>rulers</u> of the darkness of this world, against spiritual wickedness in high places. KJV emphasis mine*

Principalities power and rulers are spiritual positions in Satan's demonic chain of command. Prayer mapping is understanding the principle of warfare that two opposing sides are always in the process of taking and holding ground. Daniel's prayer antagonized the demonic prince over Persia. Satan had already assigned his principalities over geographical areas on the earth. He still does the same thing today. This is more self-evident than you may realize. For instance, New York City is ruled by power barons and greed for money. It is the financial capital of the world. Even the Islamic terrorist realized this fact in their warfare against America. They believed taking down the World Trade Center would impact the world financial system. They were correct. San Francisco is well known for what Galatians 5 calls sexual perversion, promiscuity and lasciviousness. Hollywood is controlled by it pretentious amoral lifestyle. Name any big city in America and you probably can identify the spirit that controls it.

When you practice spiritual mapping you go even deeper than the headlines. You research the history of the city or region you live in. Specifically, you look for who were the founding fathers of the city/community. Who were the influential politicians? What significant historical events took place, religious, politically, culturally, and economically? When you discover these people, events and activities, you will be surprised to see a pattern. This pattern is not coincidental, but spiritual. So to the degree these people, events and activities were and/or are anti-God's agenda, you must pray against the spirits that persist to continue its anti-kingdom agenda. Before Daniel could get an answer, God had to defeat the enemy over his region. God dispatched Michael to release his answer to Daniel's prayer. The rest, as they say, is history.

So it is with each local church. Each church has a part of God's overall agenda to advance in a particular region. When it does its research, the church will find some spiritual forces in place to stop its particular vision given to them by God. Once discovered, its intercessors must always war in prayer against those principalities. They simply use the word of God against the enemy and take back the spiritual territory.

In southern Illinois, St. Louis, MO, Metro East region where New Life is located, the following spiritual mapping has been done.

Historical strongholds that were revealed:

- The race riot of 1917 in East St. Louis.
- East St. Louis' long history of corruption.
- Up the hill, down the hill rhetoric about blacks not able to get housing east of East St. Louis and the inferiority of blacks who live "down the hill".
- Long history of a poverty spirit (culturally, spiritually, financially, economically, etc.).
- St. Louis – the gateway to the west has a transitory non-committed spirit – people known for "going through" here to get somewhere else – The Arch - Gateway to the West looking for gold, land, better life, or the gateway between southerners moving north up the Mississippi River to Chicago.

PRAYER AS A WEAPON FOR SPIRITUAL WARFARE

Despite the spiritual history, you have the power to take spiritual authority over all things that the enemy has set up to keep your church from pursuing the destiny God has for you.

Not only is this done corporately as a church, this is done on a personal level. Review your family tree and history. When you discover a pattern of diseases and illness or behavior in your family, take back your personal spiritual territory. What traps have been set in the spirit realm by Satan that you have seen manifest generation after generation? What kind of prayer mapping do you need to do to stop the "generational curse" that is trying to hinder you? Find scripture and God's promises that counter the enemy and pray them over your life. Reclaim the spiritual territory in your life. Let's look at another biblical example of spiritual mapping found in the story of Balaam.

Balaam the Children of Israel and God's Promises

- *Numbers 23:13-21: 13 Then Balak said to him, "Come with me to <u>another</u> place where you can see them; you will see only a part but not all of them. <u>And from there, curse them for me</u>." 14 So he took him to the <u>field of Zophim</u> on the <u>top of Pisgah</u>, and there he built seven altars and offered a bull and a ram on each altar. 15 Balaam said to Balak, "Stay here beside your offering while I meet with him over there." <u>16 The LORD met with Balaam</u> and put a message in his mouth and said, "Go back to Balak and give him this message." 17 So he went to him and found him standing beside his offering, with the princes of Moab. Balak asked him, "What did the LORD say?" 18 Then he uttered his oracle: "Arise, Balak, and listen; hear me, son of Zippor. 19 God is not a man, that he should lie, nor a son of man, that he should change his mind. Does* *he speak and then not act? Does he promise and not fulfill? 20 I have received a command to bless; he has blessed, <u>and I cannot change it</u>. 21 "No misfortune is seen in Jacob, no misery observed in Israel. The <u>LORD their God is with them</u>; the shout of the King is among them.*

This is what is going on in the context of this text. The children of Israel have been in the wilderness 38 years. They are, of course, a couple years from the Promised Land. They have settled down next to the Moabites.

There is nowhere in the text that Israel's intent is to attack the Moabites and take their land. Remember, the Israelites are on their way to the Promised Land. They have no interest in the Moabites' territory, but because God has given them one victory after another, not to mention clothes, food, and drink, the Moabites are intimidated. Israel can't help it if they serve a victorious God who delights in making his people victorious. The Israelites cannot be blamed for following a loving God who guided them with a pillar of cloud by day and a pillar of fire by night. They must walk in their victory and walk out their victory. But that kind of lifestyle will intimidate people. So the king of Moab orders Balaam to prophesy a curse on them.

There is a hit out on your victory and the territory you won

- *Numbers 22:5-6: 5 …sent messengers to summon Balaam son of Beor, who was at Pethor, near the River, [a] in his native land. Balak said: "A people has come out of Egypt; they cover the face of the land and have settled next to me. 6 <u>Now come and put a curse on these people</u>, because they are too powerful for me. Perhaps then I will* *be able to defeat them and drive them out of the country. For I know that those you bless are blessed, and those you curse are cursed."*

Balaam is the hit man ordered to stop Israel from advancing into their promised territory. And with most hit men, they are very capable of doing their job. I know, up to now, you may have heard preachers portray Balaam as a foolish false prophet who needs a donkey to tell him what to do. You are sadly mistaken. As I said, hit men are very capable of carrying out their assigned tasks. Balaam is no different – he is like Tom Cruise in the movie, "Collateral". He is armed and dangerous. He is ready to kill Israel's victory and he won't be stopped. Why do I say that? Balaam comes from a family of people who have a history of putting curses on individuals, families, and nations – whatever the person who hires them wants and can pay for. They are for hire like assassins.

Balaam is from Pethor. This is a city by the Euphrates River. This is near the great ancient city of Mair. In 1933, archeologists discovered a vast number of ancient tablets with complex incantations on them. Archeologists say this confirms there was a powerful cult of diviners that lived there who were hired to put curses on people. They were very successful at it. Pethor was known for its "Baru," - "Priest-Diviners," sorcerers, magicians, and soothsayers. It is believed that Balaam was from a long line of celebrated soothsayers or diviners, and that he and his family had made their living for several generations cursing or blessing other people. Their family reputation was known throughout the entire region. If anyone wanted anyone else cursed, they would send for someone from Balaam's family, because they were the best in the world at cursing people, territories, regions and nations – in other words, they conducted spiritual mapping. It was their family trade. They passed it down and gave their sons names that went along with their trade, like "Burning," and "Devourer." These guys—regardless of the requestor's religion or political stripe—would, for a price, do their auguries, or say their incantations, make the sacrifices or whatever for some particular god, and then they would curse the other party in the name of that god.

So, that was what King Balak was doing. He was sending for the most renowned Spiritual Mapper in the known world—Balaam—to come and curse Israel. King Balak had heard about all the things that God had done for Israel. He needed the very best, because he was going up against the very best – the God of Abraham, Isaac and Jacob. He was going up against the God who could rain manna down from heaven every day for 38 years. He was a God who could bring 10 plagues upon the people of Egypt, and could find water in the desert for 1.5 to 3 million people.

The biblical historians tell us they were adept at tapping into the spirit realm and telling evil spirits to do what they wanted. Now you understand why Balaam was not "taken aback" to talk to a donkey. He was used to spirits of all kinds.

- *Numbers 22:28-31: 28 Then the LORD opened the donkey's mouth, and she said to Balaam, "What have I done to you to make you beat me these three times?" 29 Balaam answered the donkey, "You have made a fool of me! If I had a sword in my hand, I would kill you right now." 30 The donkey said to Balaam, "Am I not your own donkey, which you have always ridden to this day? Have I been in the habit of doing this to you?" "No," he said. 31 Then the LORD opened Balaam's eyes, and he saw the angel of the LORD standing in the road with his sword drawn. So he bowed low and fell facedown.* He was used to talking to spirits in whatever manifestation.

Understand something – the territory God has given you is intimidating. It will cause the enemy to want to kill, steal and destroy your territory. Don't ignore the enemy. He has power, deception, dismay, discouragement, delay, dirt, destruction…but he does not have authority to take what belongs to you. Start spiritual mapping and remember the following:

Your Victory is Irrevocable

- *Numbers 23:19-20: 19 God is not a man, that he should lie, nor a son of man, that he should change his mind. Does he speak and then not act? Does he promise and not fulfill? <u>20 I have received a command to bless; he has blessed, and I cannot change it.</u>*

You have heard this quoted many times, but fail to connect it to the context. Why does Balaam say he could not change or revoke the Israelites victory or blessings? Remember, Balaam lived at Pethor. Pethor has made some historians wonder, but they think they know where it is. It is 400 miles to the north of Moab on the banks of the Euphrates River, 12 miles south of Carchemish. This region was historically heavily contested by the enemy. Balaam lived just a stone's throw away from this area. This is very important to know, because we're getting back to a connection between Abraham and Balaam. Haran is the homeland of Abraham. Haran is only 50 miles or less away. This is approximately the same territory the Israelites find themselves in and their enemies come from; it is the same place God commanded a blessing and victory over them hundreds of years before hand. So Balaam could not go against what God authorized and mapped out in the spirit realm well before Balaam's time.

- *Number 24:13-14: 13 'Even if Balak gave me his palace filled with silver and gold, I could not do anything of my own accord, good or bad, to go beyond the command of the LORD -and I must say only what the LORD says?' 14 Now I am going back to my people, but come, let me warn you of what this people will do to your people in days to come.*

In the story of Balaam, we see that Balaam was prevented from carrying out his prophesy because God had already placed a blessing on Israel and the territory. God had mapped out the territory. You must always be acutely aware of what God has said about you and your future. Jeremiah 29:11 says it best: *"For I know the plans I have for you,"* declares the LORD, *"plans to prosper you and not to harm you, plans to give you hope and a future."* NIV God has mapped out your victories for your success long before you were born.

My mother knew the plans God had for my life. She would tell me long before I went to college that I would preach before thousands. I have and I do. So, before she would release me to adulthood that morning I saw her praying, she began to spiritually map out my future and bring it in line with what God had in store for me. As I got older and began to encounter the princes of Persia in college, marriage and in my military career, I would call home for prayer. My mother would say, "Let me call the prayer warriors and son, remember – God is still on the throne." As long as God is on the throne, he is taking territory on our behalf.

In chapter three I shared my story of how the Lord answered my prayers to go to seminary, which was territory Satan did not want me to have. The part of the story I did not share was how I fought to become a chaplain. You see, my childhood hopes and dream were to be an Air Force (AF) chaplain, and eventually pastor a large, successful church. Seminary was the step I needed before I could do that. When I attended seminary, I worked for a hateful person who tried to ensure my AF career was quashed. He was a "Prince of Persia" personified, but he did not know my desire to become a chaplain, so he signed off on my tuition assistance to go to seminary. He never inquired what classes I was taking. I endured his hateful rants, diatribes and demeaning tirades about my work because I knew God had a plan for my life and territory for me to possess. I got orders to Germany again, just like before, so I knew God was up to something. I told the AF I didn't want to go. The AF said I either accept the orders or resign. In an instant my livelihood would be gone with a house payment, two car payments, and a wife and baby girl. I told my boss I wanted to be a chaplain. They were stunned and tried to block my path, and force me to resign. I went to the AF Chief of Chaplains and made my case.

They said there were too many regulations and rules that prevented me from transferring from my career field into the chaplaincy. Besides, I didn't have the required seminary degree, but they would try to help if my present career field would cooperate. My supervisor, commander and career field headquarters was against transfer. They put every stumbling block in my way. They made it clear I had burned my bridge to stay in the career field and they weren't going to release me. In other words, they were not happy to just curse my territory, they wanted to destroy me. I prayed. My mother prayed. Weeks went by. Then I received a call from my career field headquarters. The same person who was blocking my way said he found a loophole in the regulations. The very person who said it would never happen and tried to stop my transfer was now the chief proponent of it. I applied to transfer into the chaplaincy under an obscure rule #13 – miscellaneous.

But that's not all. The chaplaincy originally said I needed my seminary degree. Then they inexplicably said all I needed was 90 graduate semester hours. I had 84 – some of which I got while stationed in Korea (Remember I didn't get promoted; my assignment to Germany was cancelled and then went to Korea). The AF chaplaincy said they wanted me to be a chaplain. They changed all the rules and what they couldn't change, they waived. They said we will station you close to a seminary so you can finish your seminary degree. One day I was an AF support officer. The next day I was a chaplain. I was only the second person in AF history to do that. I was even commissioned a chaplain without a seminary degree.

The AF assigned me to Moody AFB in Valdosta, GA, so I could commute to Atlanta to complete my six hours at Interdenominational Theological Center (ITC). All of this was done so I could fulfill the destiny in my life and claim the territory my mother mapped out 13 years earlier. What Satan tried to stop, he couldn't. The AF could not reverse the blessing God ordained. The very persons pronouncing a curse over me turned around and blessed me. You see if I had not become a chaplain, I would have ended my career. I would not have come to Scott AFB in the Metro East of St. Louis. I would have never started New Life. All this is as a result of spiritual mapping. Need I say more? This church would only be in heaven and not a reality operating on earth. In less than five years, 28 people grew to over 2,300 and built an over six-million-dollar New Life Campus to the glory of God!!

Chapter Study Guide

1. What illnesses, bad behavior, and problems have consistently plagued your family?

2. What city/community do you live in?

3. Do you know the history of your location?

4. What possible prayers have not been answered due to your failure to spiritually map your life or region?

5. List the territory you want to take for the kingdom, both personally and for your church?

6. Write a personal prayer that clearly maps out the territory you believe God has for you.

PRAYER ANSWERS GUARANTEED!

7. Write a prayer that clearly maps out and agrees with the territory you believe God has for your church. You may want to consult your pastor.

Conclusion

At this point in the book you should understand how to pray to get guaranteed answers. You should have several written prayers that will be springboards to launch you into a powerful prayer life.

You should understand your base knowledge of prayer and where you need to improve. Additionally, you should be able to find scriptures of God's promises to match your prayer request. After learning how to pray God's word you can map out a prayer strategy to take the territory God has for you. Remember, prayer without faith will not result in much of anything. *Hebrews 11:6, ...and without faith it is impossible to please God, because anyone who comes to him must believe that he exists and that he rewards those who earnestly seek him.*

As you begin this new approach to prayer, many doubters will try to discourage you. They will say things like, God does always answer prayer with yes, no or wait. Ignore their ignorance. When the answer according to the word of God does not come right away, don't stop. Ask God for strength, joy and power until the answer comes. Remember, God cares deeply about everything that concerns you and wants to stay in constant communication

PRAYER ANSWERS GUARANTEED!

with you. Prayer is God's secondary means, after the Bible, of keeping the lines of communication open to strengthen our relationship with him. Based on that, we will get answers from God guaranteed. Pray continually and without ceasing a life of peace, power and prosperity awaits you!

If you have read this book but have never prayed the simplest prayer of all – the sinner's prayer – then let me give you this opportunity. God will answer it. It's as simple as ABC.

A. Lord, I **a**dmit I am a sinner in need of a Savior. I am sorry and repent for sinning against you.
B. Lord, I **b**elieve Jesus Christ is your only begotten son who lived, was crucified, died and was raised on the third day, and ascended into heaven. Now Jesus sits on the right hand of the father and he is my Savior.
C. Lord, I **c**onfess now what my heart believes.

Welcome to the family of God! Start praying… God is ready to communicate.

LaVergne, TN USA
12 October 2009
160532LV00001B/6/P